KU-191-219

THE ENGLISH NOVELISTS
General Editor:
HERBERT VAN THAL

BARRIE
AND THE
KAILYARD SCHOOL

Uniform with this Volume:

THE BRONTËS by Phyllis Bentley.
SAMUEL BUTLER by G. D. H. Cole.
HENRY FIELDING by Elizabeth Jenkins.
ROBERT LOUIS STEVENSON by Lettice Cooper.
BULWER-LYTTON by The Earl of Lytton, K.G.
RUDYARD KIPLING by Rupert Croft-Cooke.
ARNOLD BENNETT by Walter Allen.
SIR WALTER SCOTT by Una Pope-Hennessy.
MRS. GASKELL by Yvonne ffrench.
ANTHONY TROLLOPE by Beatrice Curtis Brown.
MARIA EDGEWORTH by P. H. Newby.
MRS. EWING, MRS. MOLESWORTH, MRS. HODGSON BURNETT by Marghanita Laski.
GEORGE BORROW by Martin Armstrong.
D. H. LAWRENCE by Anthony West.
H. G. WELLS by Norman Nicholson.
JANE AUSTEN by Margaret Kennedy.
RONALD FIRBANK by Jocelyn Brooke.
SHERIDAN LE FANU by Nelson Browne.

BARRIE
AND THE
KAILYARD SCHOOL

by

GEORGE BLAKE

LONDON
ARTHUR BARKER LTD.

First published 1951

Printed in Great Britain by
THE CAMPFIELD PRESS, ST. ALBANS
FOR ARTHUR BARKER LTD., 30 MUSEUM STREET, LONDON, W.C.1

This short study is respectfully dedicated
to Two Master Librarians

John Dunlop of the Mitchell Library, Glasgow,

and

Herbert Henderson of the Greenock Library,

indefatigable and endlessly patient in
research on behalf of indolent authors.

CHAPTER I

THE novelist's fundamental concern is with the human soul; its many trials and its occasional triumphs, its humours, its follies, its gropings and its generosities. He seeks to portray the ways of universal man from China to Peru. Dickens and Dostoievsky, Scott and Cervantes, Balzac, Thackeray, Flaubert and the rest were all, in their various ways, seeking to catch and pin down their own fleeting glimpses of the Truth about Human Life in general.

Most of us require of the novelist, however, that he shall state his case in interesting and valid human terms. Especially, we look to him to create an " atmosphere," to describe the scene against which his puppets move, and to account for the manners, dialects and even the costumes of the period and place in which his tale is set. We expect him, in his task of creating " the willing suspension of disbelief," to be something of a social historian as well. His work must be to some extent what is nowadays called " documentary " in character.

The novelists are the reporters and colourists of history. If a foreign friend were eager to study, say, the conditions of the poor in England in the early nineteenth century, one would refer him to the works of Dickens and Mrs. Gaskell as well as to the tomes of the formal historians. We find more in Chekov than the dissection of a feckless society; we are enchanted by his revelation of a strange, foreign scene and, in the good Scots phrase, foreign " weys o' daein' "—ways of doing. British and American writers have written brilliantly about the French people, but we go to Balzac and

Flaubert and de Maupassant for the pictorial background, the inside story. Roughly speaking, for nearly two centuries the novelists discharged the social task now being assumed by the cine-camera. . . . It is perhaps hardly relevant, but the development of the film may have some bearing on the present uneasy status of the novel as an art-form.

If, then, we look to fiction to help our understanding of unvisited scenes and alien modes of thought and custom, what impression of Scottish life and character have non-Scottish readers got from the Scottish novelists? The various answers to this question are all surprising and mostly fantastic.

Most people know that modern, workaday Scotland is as far from being a paradise for clansmen in kilts, with heather trimmings and stags at eve, as it is from being a pantomime land of comedians, in which haggis, haddocks, bagpipes, whisky and an ill-tempered God affect in their various ways the souls of its pawky inhabitants. The daily newspaper reading of the most self-centred Cockney should have convinced him by now that Scotland is, in its most urgent aspect, a highly-industrialized country, a sort of British Ruhr, with a great productivity of " heavy " goods—coal, ships, steel—square mile upon square mile of slum, a passionate public interest in professional football and in the hazards of distant English racecourses, a lot of dog-racing tracks, and a rapidly decreasing respect for the authority of the Parish Minister.

The fact is that the Industrial Revolution knocked the old Scotland sideways, with a violence in both the process and the consequences unexampled. A strange series of historical accidents brought it about that a certain amount of native genius, and certain natural supplies of raw materials, turned the Clyde Valley almost overnight into a Black Country. Highland folk of the old Celtic tradition flocked to pick up gold in the streets of Glasgow; Irish peasants, their priests arriving with them, were induced by subsidy to come across and dig the sewers and navvy on the new railway lines. Even Lithuanians were at one stage persuaded (D.P.'s of the nineteenth century) to immigrate and help to solve the man-power problems of an expanding area. Two-thirds of the population of Scotland is now confined within the boundaries of four cities. Fully one-half is imprisoned within the narrow belt of low-lying " connurbation " that stretches untidily, if with a few pleasant gaps, across the waist of the country from Dundee, on the east, to Greenock on the west.

The bulk of the Scottish people were thus condemned to a purely urban, sophisticated, and mainly ugly sort of life during the nineteenth century. A really dramatic, often beastly, revolution was taking place. And what had the Scottish novelists to say about it? The answer is—nothing, or as nearly nothing as makes no matter. They might as well have been living in Illyria as in the agonized country of their birth.

Now, this is a very strange thing altogether. It almost suggests a sort of national infantilism. The Scots are not a wholly unintelligent race. They are generally credited with the faculty of realism. But there it is—their representative writers during the nineteenth century had hardly a single word to say about the revolution that was so dramatically over-taking their natural, national " weys o' daein'." I have been at pains in my lifetime to try to dig out literary traces of an awareness of what was happening to Scotland during that period. Only two have rewarded a patient endeavour. One is a completely forgotten but remarkably solid novel called *St. Mungo's City*, by Sarah Tytler, with some excellent detail about Glasgow's textile industry in the early nineteenth century, and one splendid chapter about a cruise on the Firth of Clyde in a popular steamboat. Then the late Frederick Niven made a pass at a Scottish " novel of manners " with *The Justice of the Peace*, a more than worthy picture of conditions in a Glasgow warehouse and of *bourgeois* society in the still-expanding city. The rest is silence, almost as if it were a conspiracy of silence.

The English novelists were never so indifferent to what was happening in the North and the Midlands of their green and pleasant land. Industry and its effects were the themes of gifted writers from Mrs. Gaskell to D. H. Lawrence; the transition from the serfdom of the fields to the blacker slavery of the mills so stirred the English social conscience that even Dickens found it difficult to be funny in *Hard Times*. The absence of a similar interest in Scotland, where the process was relatively so much more revolutionary, is the subject for a debate that might fill a volume; and it would have to be a profound study of the Scottish *ethos*. Two or three lines of thought may be briefly suggested.

It must, I think, be taken for granted that, though Edinburgh sheltered an able and influential literary circle towards the end of the eighteenth century, the general literary culture of Scotland was in a sad state of decline after two centuries of the influence of a fundamentalist Kirk. The educational system of Scotland has often enough been held up as a model of its kind, but that is to overrate the importance of the kind. It was an admirable parochial system of what is nowadays called Primary education, and it diffused a relatively high standard of literacy; but if it also produced scholars out of the " lads o' pairts," their culture was apt to be classical and mathematical, taking a poor view of cloud-capp'd towers and gorgeous palaces. It is probable that the Kirk would have frowned upon, and openly rebuked, a native John Keats for the worldliness of his imagery; but it is more to the point that Scottish conditions at the period could hardly have favoured the emergence of a Keats at all. Burns was the natural voice of a predominantly peasant people; and even the classical pundits of Edinburgh advised the author of the " Ode to a Grecian Urn " to go back to his gallipots.

Another explanation—probably just another factor—is that Scotland was too swiftly, and too brutally, overwhelmed by the Industrial Revolution. The Nationalist might say, and with some reason, that the Scot found in the new metal trades a means of expression he had lacked since his national identity was finally lost with the Union of the Parliaments in 1707. He would proceed to argue, again with sense, that the native energies were too thoroughly absorbed in the expansion to allow of adequate literary expression. He might go on to maintain, a trifle less confidently, that the native writers who neglected the industrial factor altogether and wrote prettily of parochial life were really harking back to the idyllic state of their country in its condition of independence. I may be allowed to help the Nationalist in this argument by pointing out that, with the departure of the Scottish nobility for the Court of St. James's after the Union of the Crowns in 1603 (except in so far as they had to make token appearances in their hereditary lands), the contemporary system of patronage was largely denied the native writer.

It has been ably argued, again, that the enormous influence of Walter Scott interposed a high wall of Gothic assumptions between the Scottish artist and his proper objectives; dramatizing and pictorializing, and not very accurately at that, a dead and really brutal past in both medieval England and the Scottish Highlands under the clan system. It is reasonably added that the elegant romanticism of Robert Louis Stevenson had a distracting effect on the few literary artists of a race that is apt to this day to envy precisely such ease as had seemed to enable R. L. S. to rejoin the stream of the general European culture.

This is an attractive position, but it seems to me to be perilously undermined by the fact that Scott was capable of such tales as *The Antiquary* and *The Heart of Midlothian*, and by a suspicion that if his Scottish followers had striven to emulate the thoroughly native spirit in which the man could write like a fairy when he was in the mood, then the later history of the novel in Scotland might have been much happier. And if we are all very superior about Stevenson's tricks of style and Brook Street brilliance, it is still a pity that more of his successors could not, or would not, strive to better *Thrawn Janet*, the fragment of *Weir of Hermiston* (though that is apt to be conventionally overpraised) and even certain passages of pure and thoroughly Scottish writing in the romances of *Kidnapped* and *Catriona* and *The Master of Ballantrae*.

There is no doubt at all, however, that a basic Scottish instinct is towards romance. It may be the pervasive Celtic blood, in the traditional way of putting it; it may be, in a harsher reading, the escapism of a defeated and absorbed people. It is certain that Scott and Stevenson gave the Scottish output of fiction its slant during the nineteenth century. We should also note, with due humility, that they were the most fully-equipped novelists Scotland had produced since Tobias Smollett. This is not to forget John Galt, of whom we shall have something to say shortly.

The bulk of Scottish fiction during the nineteenth century thus fell into either of two categories: the domestic or parochial on the one hand, the romantic on the other. The novel of manners did not develop at all, in spite of the inclination that way of Susan Ferrier; and we might safely say there were few of the manners of an established society to write about. As we have seen, the industrial fret was completely ignored. The Scots storyteller either followed Scott and Stevenson through the heather with a claymore at his belt, or he lingered round the bonnie brier bush, telling sweet, amusing little stories of bucolic intrigue as seen through the windows of the Presbyterian manse.

Our concern here is with the members of the latter school, but we should note that even the avowed Romantics could return on occasion from the moors and corries to the safer territory about the parish pump. Of these Romantics (and the term is used only for convenience) Neil Munro and John Buchan are the only figures that need concern us: the first a Gaelic-speaking Highlander, the second a Lowlander with Border affiliations.

Neil Munro (1864–1930) passed his young life in the Highlands, and that in a lovely region where the heroic legends really did survive into his boyhood. He was reared under the walls of a duke's castle; the long memory of the clan system informed his infancy. His virtues as a storyteller of the small wars of the Highlands resided in the ability to keep a romantic story moving, in an alluring prose style (based largely on the literal translation of Gaelic into English), in a rare feeling for the humours of human intercourse among males, and in a poet's eye for scenery. His limitations were lack of range and a quite astonishing indifference to, or modesty regarding, females, so that his womenfolk are lay figures and his version of a given society correspondingly incomplete.

All that may seem perhaps a little beside our present point, but it is put forward here with deliberation. For throughout most of his working life Neil Munro was engaged in journalism in Glasgow, fully aware of what was going on in the overcrowded city about him and of what it portended for the Scotland he loved in its romantic aspects. It requires more than the easy use of the word " escapism " to account for these facts. The dreadful dichotomy in the soul of the gifted Scot was never more painfully illustrated. And when Neil Munro tired of the Highlands as a subject, or felt the need to change the direction of his attack in the light of changing literary fashion, or was simply worn out by a long and singularly brilliant career in journalism—then he did not write about the majority problems of the Clyde basin (a region he knew like the back of his hand) but simply took, as in *The Daft Days*, to a domestic and " pawky " setting, even if it was in the Highlands and not somewhere in the potato-growing region of Drumtochty.

The case of John Buchan, first Lord Tweedsmuir, is similar, though this fantastically able man had at once a wider range and somewhat less scrupulous artistic ideals than Munro. As a writer of fiction (as distinct from his poetic and scholarly exercises) he started at an early age in the Stevensonian vein, and he remained Stevensonian in general quality and approach even when he had hit on the popular formula of the Mr. Standfast series, but it is to the present point that when invention flagged, and his anecdote could not be raised to the Common Room level he venerated, he would return anon to the pawky simplicities of village life as seen from his father's Free Kirk manse.

One is tempted to linger over the case of John Buchan. It was a very remarkable one of the diffusion of the highest talents, like that of William Robertson Nicoll, which we shall be considering shortly, with versatility in several literary forms apparently marching, but really contending, with administrative abilities and political ambition. A Scottish writer of genius might take John Buchan as the perfect specimen of the " lad o' pairts " and hew out of the abundant material, including his autobiography, a saga in the manner of *Jean Christophe*. It would be, rightly handled, a startling study of the intrusion of Scottish ability in Imperial affairs; it might turn out to be a case of genius *manqué*. Being here humbly concerned with literary values, we note merely the characteristic overlap as between romance and sentiment in the make-up of the nineteenth-century novelists of Scotland. It was perhaps most clearly visible in the works of S. R. Crockett, who could gossip round the parish pump with the best like any old wifie, and could also follow Stevenson, if in a somewhat embarrassing *pastiche* of the eighteenth-century manner, in such excellent tales of adventure as *The Raiders* and *Men of the Moss Hags*.

Once we have dealt, however, with a group of Scottish writers on three grades of excellence—Scott on the topmost tier, Stevenson on a lower level, Neil Munro and John Buchan derivatively with them but below decks in the larger assessment of these matters—we are left with a collection of small fry: the men of what has been called the Kailyard School. James Matthew Barrie excepted, none of these was anything but a reasonably competent commercial novelist.

The staggering fact remains that Scotland, with most of its people imprisoned in cities and confined to slums of the foulest order, was most popularly represented by these bucolic comedians for nearly three decades on end. Throughout three decades of peace and prosperity they presented the

English and the American reader with a picture of their country as a sort of collection of picturesque rural parishes peopled by " pawky " and/or " nippy " characters. They provided the library public with its necessary meed of the " quaint." They did not know, or they dodged, the terrible facts of overcrowding on the one hand and, on the other (though this was surely germane to their subject), rural depopulation at an alarming rate. Their work was genteel, patronizing: really a queer sort of toadying to the old traditions of Toryism, in which " the lower classes " are the honest, feckless, delightful friends of their superiors in education and financial resource. They held up their fellow-countrymen as comic characters for the amusement of the foreigner. It was as if the whole life and culture of England were to be represented by the antics of Zummerzet yokels; as if all the United States were typified by Mrs. Wiggs's cabbage-patch.

It is an interesting fact that the literatures of domesticity and rustic humour in the States and in Scotland, relatively primitive communities, are classified according to the same symbol. For a kailyard is a cabbage-patch, even if the kail, or kale, of Scotland are the curly greens of England, the humblest of the domestic vegetables. The term suggests immediately the rural cottage and its modest kitchen garden, a sort of inner shrine of decent living in pious poverty; it admirably suggests the limited range of this school of fiction. As to its provenance, that is fairly obvious. For a motto for his immensely popular *Beside the Bonnie Brier Bush*, the clergyman who called himself " Ian Maclaren " chose two lines from a Scots country song:

> " There grows a bonnie brier bush in our kail-yard,
> And white are the blossoms on't in our kail-yard."

Who can blame the surfeited reviewer of the period for seizing on the phrase and elevating this prevalent fashion in fiction, even with malicious intention, to the dignity of the Kailyard School?

Who first used it is a question of some interest. The O.E.D. reports that the earliest use of the term was in the title of an article contributed by J. H. Millar to W. E. Henley's *New Review* in 1895, and Millar (of whom we shall hear more anon) declares in a footnote to p. 511 of his *Literary History of Scotland:*

> " It is betraying no secret to mention that for this happy nickname, which has obtained so much currency, the world is indebted to Mr. W. E. Henley and to no one else."

But here Millar seems to do himself an injustice, for in the course of his article—which brilliantly pillories the Kailyard men and leaves them shivering in their shirt-tails—he has the sentence:

> " It is a fact that J. M. Barrie is fairly entitled to look upon himself as *pars magna* if not *pars maxima* of the kailyard movement; "

so that, unless Millar had caught the phrase from Henley in private talk or correspondence beforehand, we may assume that the latter had the ordinary editorial wit to pick out the telling locution from his contributor's article and give it the emphasis of a headline, honours being thus fairly even.

As for the couplet quoted by " Ian Maclaren," it is from an old song that was done up by Burns and contributed by him to " Johnson's Museum," with the air picked up from the singing of a country girl.

There was nothing new, or anything in the least surprising, in the concentration of Scottish novelists on village and small-town humours. Outside the dropsical industrial concentration, Scotland still is a country of small towns, each remarkably isolated in its prides and prejudices by the relative difficulty of communications. The basic culture is still parochial, in the best sense of that word of fluctuating values, and Scots writers of limited range are quite likely to go on drooling about the Kailyard for a long time to come. It is often said, a thought loosely, that John Galt was the ancient father of the Kailyard School. The reference is to his *Annals of the Parish*, and this was indeed the record of a limited parochial experience. But there are in the *Annals* a bite and a roughness that would have scared the wits out of the escapists of the Victorian period; and Galt at his best could have written most of the Kailyard men (Barrie always excluded) off the map in a couple of his taut pages.

We face now the fact that, nearly a century too late, a small group of sentimental, if gifted, Scots gratified Victorian sentimentality by representing the real life of their country in terms that were quite hopelessly out of date for all practical purposes. At the same time, we must try to see that they were not wilfully dishonest. They were perhaps the victims of the chronic Scots disease of nostalgia, of the urge to escape back into the comprehensible conditions of their original, independent state and away from the new, incomprehensible turmoils of the industrial age. It is above all significant that the successful practitioners were mostly ordained ministers of one of the numerous Scottish Churches—the Free Church—and that the one who was not, James Matthew Barrie, adhered to the Free Church and dealt largely in scenes from clerical life.

They were "Ian Maclaren," the Rev. John Watson, D.D. (1850–1907), the Rev. Samuel Rutherford Crockett (1860–1914) and Barrie (1860–1937). With these, for reasons about to be explained, there must be bracketed the name of Sir William Robertson Nicoll (1851–1923).

The observant reader will note that these were all children of a vintage decade, the sixth of the nineteenth century.

CHAPTER II

THE influence of the Presbyterian ministry on Scottish life and character was very great throughout at least three centuries. The authority of the Kirk in its various denominations was based primarily on the power of the Kirk Session to sit in judgment on sinners and rebuke them in the sight of the congregation; it was assisted in authority by the fidelity of a largely peasant folk to a Fundamentalist type of belief. Thus the parish minister, as preses of the Session, the congregational governing body, could be feared as well as respected. He possessed the power of calling down hell-fire on the recalcitrant and quite a lot of decisive social sanctions as well.

It is absurd, of course, to think of the Kirk in its days of dominance as a black oppressor of joy in living. John Galt's picture of life in an eighteenth-century parish and manse glows with kindliness. The clerical error, as we see it now, was to repress the people's natural artistic inclinations in the name of Sabbath observance and to confuse, for instance, the aims of the drama with the worldliness of the playhouse. All this was in keeping with the notorious literal-mindedness of the Scot; it was indeed a fairly straight case of cause and effect. The close reading of Calvin's teachings did check the people's natural instincts of self-expression. The Kirk forced them to concentrate on and, if they must, sing about the domestic joys and virtues. Hence the couthy, cosy nature of so much Scottish song; hence the paradox whereby that wild and vivid character, Robert Burns (who scarified the holy men in his "Address to the Unco Guid"), could in another mood declare, with tears of glycerine moving slowly down his cheeks, that

> "To make a happy fireside clime
> To weans and wife,—
> That's the true pathos and sublime
> Of human life."

At the same time, especially before the development of political consciousness and local government, the manse of the rural parish was the fount of educated advice and kindly aid to poor, simple folk in trouble. Not only the Roman Catholics have the technique of the confessional. Especially as the pure milk of Calvinism began to taste a trifle sour with the advance of Liberalism in the nineteenth century, the parish minister in Scotland tended to shed his inquisitorial status and to become the gentle shepherd, though still secure in local authority. It was in this idyllic period that the Kailyard School of Scottish novelists most greatly flourished, producing the blooms of an Indian summer, even if most of the Scots folk were already huddled in slums and international taste in literature had got far beyond the bumbling of peasants round their various parish pumps. And there were plenty of the city-imprisoned millions to delight nostalgically in their pretty tales.

The Scottish clergy had one other subtle but vast advantage of their fellow-countrymen in the golden age of Presbyterianism. This was the near-monopoly of academic learning, and it was cherished with something of the rigour of trade unionism. It is very well to boast of the excellence of parochial education in Scotland in the old days. It did indeed produce a generally high average of literacy even in the peasant population, as we have noted, and it had the defect of catering specially for the "lad o' pairts" only: his advancement being as much the concern of the parish minister as of the dominie; but in nine cases out of ten the clever boy was urged by all about him to believe that his highest ideal should be "to wag his head in a pulpit"—a destiny which was dangled before the present writer (a most unlikely subject) even towards the end of the first decade of the twentieth century.

Thus the Kirk tended to draw a close circle about itself, just as its remote predecessors took refuge in Ogham script from the curiosities of the vulgar. It is only fair to repeat that the Scottish Churches demanded of their candidates respectable standards of academic attainment; and I for one know no consultative body, even the House of Commons, in which the level of debating power is so high and so highly polished as in the General Assembly of the Church of Scotland.

Thus and thus, however, the Scottish parish minister in the country districts had acquired by 1880 or thereabouts an enviable status. If he had lost his power as the dispenser of hell-fire and damnation, he was still the genial master of his bailiwick. If he cared little enough for what was happening in the stews of the Clyde-Forth Valley, the rural economy showed no sign as yet of breaking down. The good Queen Victoria was on the throne and had popularized Scotland in the south. Britannia ruled the waves, and nobody took much account of rebellious Zulus, Boers, Fuzzy-Wuzzies and such. All the British peoples had good reason to be well content with their international status at least; and such a man as Keir Hardie was obviously mad.

In such an age of apparent peace and plenty, with the traditional leaders of the community batting on an easy wicket, the Scots parish minister, in spite of an often miserly stipend, was on top of his little world. If he had any gift of the pen he could most amusingly and profitably display his remote charge and his comic parishioners to a large public enchanted by the variety of the British Empire, on which the sun, at that period, showed not the slightest sign of setting.

Roughly speaking, the Kailyard School of novelists came to flourish along these lines, but we do not understand the process rightly unless we see that the ripeness of the Scottish ministry for self-expression coincided with a surprising expansion of religious journalism along popular lines: the Liberal Nonconformists, in fact, beating Alfred Harmsworth and his *Daily Mail* by more than a decade. The historian of modern journalism might decide that Sir George Newnes with his *Tit-Bits* was the true originator of the new technique. Others might say that the real start was made by a queer, immensely able Scotsman called William Robertson Nicoll. Here it is argued that Robertson Nicoll fathered and mothered the Kailyard men through his special sort of editorial genius and the swift success of his *British Weekly*, not to forget his important say in the policies and decisions of the publishing house of Hodder & Stoughton.

Whether Robertson Nicoll or John Buchan was the most astonishing "lad o' pairts" produced by a Scottish manse would be a nice question for debate. Almost the only ostensible differences between them were that Buchan was certainly an artist, Nicoll much more the critic and expositor, and that Buchan enjoyed the amenities of close association with Oxford while Nicoll started straight from Aberdeen University. The similarities between the careers are almost alarming otherwise—precocity, fertility, industry, financial ability, great influence in publishing and book reviewing;

and if Buchan ended an amazing career on the proconsular level as Lord Tweedsmuir, let it not be forgotten that Nicoll, a mere Knight and Companion of Honour, was one of Lloyd George's closest confidants during the difficult last years of the First German War.

His father was the remote minister of the Free Church of Scotland in the village of Lumsden, which stands nearly 800 ft. above sea level in a hilly, hard region of Aberdeenshire, under the Cabrach. This man was the perfect bookworm. On a stipend that never exceeded £200 a year, and was often nearer £100, he accumulated a library of 17,000 volumes, said to be the largest ever got together by a Scottish clergyman on his own account; it included some five-score different editions of the Greek Testament. Thus his oldest son (whose mother had died when he was only eight) spent his childhood almost literally falling over the books that littered even the passages of the manse; and thus books were from the first those articles of the civilized life he learned most dearly to respect.

At the age of fourteen he left the village school for Aberdeen Grammar School, and six months later, being then only fifteen, entered the University of Aberdeen. This precocious entrance was not uncommon in the Scottish Universities at that period, but Robertson was still so much the Buchan loon that he did not know how to deal with the gas lighting in his lodgings. He was already so much the book-swallower that he would often quite nearly starve himself to buy a volume he coveted. This voracity for reading matter in almost any form was so persistent that (I was once told by one who knew him well) on a long train journey, even in his old age, he would dash out at every stop to buy the local newspapers. This was surely the itch of the born journalist.

In 1874, in his twenty-fourth year, Robertson Nicoll was ordained minister of the Free Church at Dufftown, in the whisky-distilling region of Banffshire. Three years later he went south to the Free Kirk at Kelso in the Border country, his health being always frail, and laboured there for some eight years. He nearly died in the autumn of 1885, but in the summer of the following year, by this time aged thirty-six, he was settled in London and launched on a busy, powerful and prosperous editorial career.

It was during his years at Kelso that Nicoll made quite a formidable start in journalism, of the religious order in the first place. He wrote frequently for the *Christian Leader*, a weekly published in Glasgow; he became religious adviser to the Edinburgh publishing firm of Macniven & Wallace; he planned and edited for the London firm of Swan, Sonnenschein the *Contemporary Pulpit*, a monthly magazine of the homilectic order; he produced two or three volumes of both devotional and literary natures; and he finally proposed to Messrs. Hodder & Stoughton, who accepted the suggestion, that he should edit for them a series of volumes to be called *The Clerical Library*. Through this last connection he became editor of that firm's important theological monthly, the *Expositor*, editing it from Kelso in the first place. Since Nicoll remained throughout these proceedings the devoted minister of a congregation of 400 souls and a preacher much in demand throughout the Free Kirk connection, he was certainly entitled to boast in later life: "I can only claim that I am one of the most industrious creatures God ever made."

No publishing firm ever made a better deal than that carried through by Mr. Stoughton in 1885, when he travelled north to Kelso in order to persuade the young minister to take over the *Expositor*. They were hiring a volcano of energy, an inexhaustible fount of sound commercial ideas with the agreeable flavour of uplift and improvement behind them.

Robertson Nicoll was born to be the last perfect expression of Liberal Nonconformity, strict in moral intention but with a very nice eye for profits. Nowadays we can only wonder at the energy of this frail man, the proliferation of his high and special talent, who, in his heyday (1901), could tell a friend by letter: "In six days I have dictated for print 35,000 words"—that is, more than the length of this study. He claimed, according to his biographer, the late T. H. Darlow, in *William Robertson Nicoll: Life and Letters* (Hodder & Stoughton, 1925), to be able to read 20,000 words in half an hour; he read at least two books a day. The renowned *hamartia* of his native Buchan could not apparently be discarded even in moments of religious and personal emotion. It is with some embarrassment one learns from the *Life and Letters* that, addressing the lady who was to become his second wife, he could write:

> "I do not know how to tell you what views I hold. But I am going to send you to-morrow two books of mine, *Ten-Minute Sermons* and *The Key of the Grave*. Both have been successful, each in its third edition, and I have put the inmost of my heart into them."

That the popular success of the volumes should take precedence of his heart-searchings in this report may be but an accident of careless writing, but the writer of a love-letter is not usually inclined to put the state of his commercial career before that of his emotions. His biographer, a shrewd and able man, says bluntly enough:

> "As he advanced in life some of his friends felt that Nicoll became more conservative in tastes and ideas—as so often happens with age. It was a more serious flaw that, as he succeeded, he grew too fond of successful men. His elder daughter admits, 'I think we were

brought up to consider unsuccessful people as not much worth knowing.' In his heart her father believed that substantially all failure is due either to stupidity or to indolence."

That last sentence is a fair enough analysis in the rough of the intolerance of the immensely competent, and we are not in any event concerned here with the matter of Robertson Nicoll's fantastically complex personality. His influence is the thing, and that, the product of his efficiency, was great in one field, even if it was only a kailyard or cabbage-patch, of creative literature.

The editorship of the *Expositor* was for the urgent Nicoll a mere opening of the door. He had been little more than a year in office when he devised, thrust upon the astonished Messrs. Hodder & Stoughton, and published with brilliant success the first number of the *British Weekly*. That was on November 5, 1886. On the first day of October, 1891, he launched the *Bookman*. Exactly two years later, to the day, *The Woman at Home* appeared to fill a long-felt want. Nicoll deliberately planned it as " a *Strand Magazine* for women," and he was careful to recruit for his band of contributors from the start the legendary Annie S. Swan, who had already worked for the *British Weekly*, and whom he was to describe as " the Scheherazade of modern story-tellers." (She was in fact a lady of great ability, modesty, humour and good sense.) Over and above the supervision of these successful adventures in journalism, Nicoll was to exercise for more than three decades a decisive and highly profitable influence in the councils of the great publishing firm of Hodder & Stoughton.

Thus power came into the hands of the loon from the remote manse in Buchan. We are chiefly concerned here with his adroit exercise of it through his darling creation, the *British Weekly*.

In its heyday this periodical was fashioned according to a fixed recipe or formula. Its opening pages were devoted to sermons or theological essays, usually contributed, to reviews of ecclesiastical works, and to news of persons and movements within the Churches, mainly the Free Churches. In its middle parts, however, it took on a literary flavour, usually with a long bookish essay by Nicoll himself, writing either as " Claudius Clear " or " A Man of Kent " (though he would often enough debate a question of pure politics), and a column of brief reviews and gossip about books and their writers. The time came when a full-length review by " Claudius Clear " could make or damn a new book; and even the column of gossip came to have immense importance in the eyes of the publishers—and to authors in their commercial capacity. The success endowed Nicoll with influence. His approval was sought, and therefore information flowed towards him. He soon became, and for more than thirty years remained, the Grand Panjandrum of popular literary journalism.

This success, this power, made him enemies. The reader with a knowledge of the period can easily enough discern that Nicoll was one of T. W. H. Crosland's chief targets in *The Unspeakable Scot.* Sir Arthur Conan Doyle, who did not relish adverse criticism, once had occasion to make public protest against what he called Nicoll's " pluralism " in reviewing, being aggrieved by a series of unfriendly notices of one of his books, which, appearing in several different quarters, bore the stamp of a single origin. The present writer may be allowed a moment of autobiography to describe his own dealings with some of Nicoll's literary remains.

These were enclosed in a large, black-japanned, lockfast metal box; and by a series of circumstances, now of no importance, this was passed to me with the appropriate keys by the late Lord Riddell, one of Nicoll's closest friends, with instructions to look through the contents and sort them out for sale, if they were marketable, for the benefit of the estate. This was in 1924.

It was a queer experience for a young man to deal with the private papers of a leader in journalism, and it was indeed an extremely curious collection of material (in both the general and the special senses) that thus passed through my hands. It was clear that, in his most influential position, Nicoll had been lent or been able to borrow all sorts of documents bearing closely on the private lives of famous literary persons, and had been canny enough to keep type-written copies of them all. That rather damp squib, the *Life of Christ*, written by Dickens for his children, was one of the few more printable items. Others were very odd indeed. A professional biographer of the post-Lytton Strachey school would have been set up for life, and his son after him, on the startling appeal of the copied documents the Rev. Dr. Nicoll had rightly kept under lock and key.

At the time, let me make it clear, I was more fascinated by a wholly blameless collection of autograph letters, dating from the early 'eighties, in which all the great British literary figures of the day, Stevenson included, confided to the young Free Kirk minister at Kelso the general intentions of their works and their methods of writing. We know now that Nicoll had projected with a younger brother a history of English Literature down to the latest times; and these were the responses of the contemporary great to his earnest inquiries for information. They were of singular bibliographical interest, and I feel that their preservation over so many years, if merely prudent, was still the not unpleasing mark of Nicoll's passionate, real interest in the mechanics and *personalia* of writing. The letters were ultimately sold at Sotheby's for a tidy sum: to whom I know not.

This, however, is to get rather far away from the special case of the *British Weekly*, its pattern and influence; and the point now is that Nicoll, an alarmingly skilful cook, saw that his recipe must include a swatch of fiction, no doubt to please the ladies of the manses. We may never know whether he bought his stories and serials to please himself or to satisfy his own acute sense of what comfortable Liberal Nonconformity would like. Bearing in mind the real acuteness of many of his judgments, particularly in his private correspondence, one inclines to conclude that he was mainly a shrewd merchant. One brief passage in Darlow's *Life and Letters* seems to convey the gist of the matter:

> " Nicoll was vexed when his daughter did not foresee at once that Mrs. Florence Barclay's books would have a big success. ' Duchesses and hymns! " he said, ' of course the books will sell.' "

At all events, much of the material now recognized as the kernel of Kailyard fiction was either serialized in the *British Weekly* in the first place or attracted to the publishing house of Hodder & Stoughton through Nicoll's influence for publication in book form. James Matthew Barrie, having first served an invaluable apprenticeship to Frederick Greenwood, of the *St. James's Gazette*, started contributing to the *British Weekly* within a few months of its establishment, using the pseudonym of " Gavin Ogilvy." The discovery of " Ian Maclaren " as a writer of emollient fiction was entirely Nicoll's affair and, as we shall see, John Watson was an established divine of middle age before he was persuaded by the editor of the *British Weekly* to turn storyteller. S. R. Crockett was not among Nicoll's discoveries, but in a

Christmas message to the paper he wrote: " The *British Weekly* said the first good word for my first book. You showed kindness unspeakable to a man unknown and discouraged. You are, sir, of the great company of the encouragers, who make the wheels of the world go round. More power to your elbow."

In the longer historical view there was nothing a great deal surprising in the emergence of the *British Weekly* or in the development and popularity of the Kailyard School. The legendary Norman MacLeod had indicated the journalistic pattern in *Good Words*; as we have seen, the cabbage-patch themes are persistent in Scottish fiction. The thesis here is simply that this particular plot of vegetables flourished most luxuriantly in the pages of the *British Weekly* under the assiduous attentions of William Robertson Nicoll. One cannot think that there would ever have been a Kailyard School without him.

CHAPTER III

WHEN considering, however ruefully, the immense popularity of the Kailyard novels and the praise they evoked from contemporary reviewers, it is well to continue to remember that most of them were written fifty years ago and more, in an age of great prosperity and self-satisfaction. The British industrial effort was near its peak. Income Tax was still at a few pence in the pound; Britannia ruled the waves; and if the bulk of the working population was still condemned to low wages and grim conditions, the middle classes, constituting the reading public, were still strong and safe and in no mood to consider the long-range political and economic implications of their prosperity. Freud, Adler and Jung were still to disturb the conventional notions of behaviour; the dire works of Karl Marx were still known to only a few cranks. Novel-reading was a more highly-popular form of light recreation than it is to-day.

The great march of classic English fiction proceeded indeed. It is an odd thought that *Jude the Obscure* and *The Time Machine*, the former marking the end of Hardy's career as a novelist, appeared in much the same publishing season as *Beside the Bonnie Brier Bush*. But of the latter quarter of a million copies were quickly sold in Britain, half a million in the States—figures so phenomenal at any period that we may wonder exactly wherein the attraction lay.

Even a lowbrow reader of to-day might probably find *Beside the Bonnie Brier Bush* a trifle cloying in its sentimentality and more than a little tedious in the primitiveness of its technique; he would certainly look for a good deal more of those elements that are nowadays grouped under the heading of Sex. There was never an orchid nor a Miss Blandish in Drumtochty, and the complete absence of plot makes the success all the more difficult to understand. " Ian Maclaren's " staggering best-seller is a rather thin collection of blameless " sketches," thinner in both physical and literary substance than Barrie's *Auld Licht Idylls*, like it only in giving the modern reader a faintly unpleasant impression of a collection of rustic oddities being exposed to the laughter of foreigners.

This is, in my submission, probably the clue to its popularity. Popular taste in the 'nineties tended towards the unusual, the quaint, the bizarre. On the more sophisticated level the bright lads of the *Yellow Book* expressed and gratified this inclination; the Kailyard men did the needful for Nonconformist taste. (It is an amusing study to compare the suave sentimentality of Henry Harland, for instance, with the blunter, but not any more dishonest, expression of the same quality in " Ian Maclaren's " works.) It seems significant that the reviewers, and even the solid critics of the period, wrote almost invariably of " dialect fiction," thus surely confessing that the adroit use of the Scots vernacular was an ingredient of popularity. It was " quaint." The smiles and tears, the little joys and sorrows of rustic characters speaking slowly and pawkily in an odd variant of English —that was, roughly speaking, the formula.

It needs no fine work with elaborate critical apparatus to demonstrate that the Rev. John Watson, D.D., was the least gifted with real literary qualities of the Kailyard triumvirate, his huge commercial success notwithstanding. It is truly remarkable that this success came to him in middle age, when he had already achieved real eminence in his ministerial career and after he had been persuaded, against his protests, into penning his little sketches of parochial life.

He was born, remarkably enough, at Manningtree, Essex, in 1850, but his parents were both of pure Highland blood: the father from the Braemar district, the mother a Gaelic-speaking Maclaren from central Perthshire. The father, an officer of the Inland Revenue, was promoted to posts of some importance in his native country and young John first attended Perth Academy and then the High School of Stirling. At the early age of sixteen, as was then the custom, he proceeded to Edinburgh University. He is described, in an excellent phrase, as being a " reluctant " student, and he remained reluctant when, having graduated in 1870, parental pressure forced him through the portals of New College, the Edinburgh theological hall of the Free Church of Scotland. He thought on his own part of studying Law; and John Watson would assuredly have made a successful advocate and, in due course, a reasonably wise judge; but after a divinity course, which included a semester at Tübingen, and without collecting any notable academic distinctions, he was licensed to preach and duly ordained as Free Kirk minister of Logiealmond, across the River Almond from that notoriously Episcopal institution, Trinity College. This pleasant Perthshire village became the " Drumtochty " of " Ian Maclaren's" highly-esteemed tales.

Impressionable critics have thought it wonderful that during such a brief tenure of office in Logiealmond—it lasted slightly less than three years—Watson should have acquired the material for several volumes. This is nonsense. The lad was brought up in Perth and Stirling, then compact market towns and full of "characters," and no doubt he had throughout the impressionable years continuous contacts with country speech and "weys o' daein'." Logiealmond was only Perth in little, the right, easily-comprehensible stage for the simple little dramas John Watson was destined to write. It is, again, more truly remarkable that his chronicles of the parish pump were written when he was a big man in the Presbyterian camp, the busy, energetic, immensely competent minister of a rich charge, in Liverpool of all places!

On his way from Logiealmond to Liverpool Watson sojourned for three years in Glasgow as associate minister of Free St. Matthew's. He was hardly happy in the face of divided responsibility and of a rich, influential and no doubt opinionated congregation, but the charge provided him with metropolitan experience and a wife from one of Glasgow's merchant families. Both were valuable assets when he came to preside, at the age of only thirty, over the affairs of Sefton Park Church, Liverpool.

Sefton Park in 1880 was a developing suburb of the great seaport. It housed a prosperous Scots colony and a number of prosperous English Nonconformists; its people were mostly substantial and serious-minded citizens. Watson's great gifts as a preacher and administrator, and the enthusiasm and shrewdness of his elders, soon turned Sefton Park Church into a stronghold of the Presbyterian Church of England. They put up a handsome and expensive building, and they made a distinct mark on the life of the city. Six Lord Mayors of Liverpool from time to time belonged to Watson's congregation. On his own part, the minister was prominent in communal affairs, an excellent citizen of his adopted town, and had in fact much to do with the foundation of Liverpool University.

His fame spread outwards. A tall man with a finely-modelled face, a thoughtful preacher with a good voice, he was in demand for pulpits all over the country. His authority grew rapidly within the inner councils of his Church, and in due course he became its Moderator. If John Watson had not also been " Ian Maclaren," we might still have heard of him as a considerable churchman of his time.

The paradox, over which a novelist might linger long enough, is that Watson remained an active, eager churchman and a busy administrator long after " Ian Maclaren " had won for him a small fortune and the possibility of a pleasant, independent way of life. But he remained the busy minister of Sefton Park for twenty-five years and resigned not long before his early death at the age of fifty-seven. He himself declared, and his biographer (the ubiquitous Robertson Nicoll) repeats, that he regarded his fantastically successful fiction as a by-product, and all the evidence does seem to show that the assertion was well founded. In that, as we shall see, he was happier than Samuel Rutherford Crockett.

It was altogether a strange case of a mature man, well settled in a profession he loved, stumbling upon, at least, material success and contemporary esteem in another. Robertson Nicoll, his ears alertly cocked as usual, had spotted Watson as one of the coming men in the theological field and first approached him as a likely contributor to the *Expositor*. In due course Watson arrived to spend a day or two at Bay Tree Lodge, Hampstead, with the editor of that grave periodical and revealed himself, outside the expository field, as a sensitive, alert Celt with great talents as a *raconteur*, full of good stories of village life in Scotland. The editor of the *British Weekly* thereupon promptly supplanted his opposite number in the chair of the *Expositor* and urged his guest to put his anecdotes in writing. Nicoll wrote afterwards:

> "The idea had never struck him, and was at first unwelcome. But I kept on persuading him. I had no success till I was accompanying him to the station, when I pressed the matter on him. Just before he said good-bye he promised to try, and in a few days the first sketch arrived."

Thus, after a few false starts, the Liverpool minister who had travelled to London to discuss "The Leading Ideas of Jesus" for the *Expositor* was committed to writing little tales of Drumtochty's pawky parishioners for the *British Weekly*. Watson declared long afterwards, and with clear sincerity, that he would never have dreamed to turning his anecdotes into fiction but for this accident; he was genuinely puzzled that Ian Maclaren became so much more famous than John Watson.

The success of the storyteller was swift and complete. The first Drumtochty sketch was published in the *British Weekly* in the week of the present writer's birth in October, 1893, and shortly the new writer was being hailed as brilliant by men of the highest standing and still invulnerable reputation for learning and taste. This last fact is important as showing that, if we smile sourly at his complacencies under the shadow of the atomic bomb, Watson-Maclaren was a true flower of his period.

Late Victorian biography was anything but candid. As applied to reverend parties it was apt to be a good deal less than that. There now exists no material by which the personality of John Watson can be freely assessed; he is embalmed in the frankincense and myrrh appropriate to a successful divine. The puzzle, however, is rendered all the more difficult by the somewhat alarming disparity between Robertson Nicoll's private and public references to his contemporaries. Thus, writing to his regular correspondent, Dr. Marcus Dods, after Watson's first visit to Bay Tree Lodge, he observed:

> " He stayed with us three nights and was very pleasant, but somehow I did not take to him so much as I expected; he was too cynical for me."

So it was a cynic who wrote *Beside the Bonnie Brier Bush*! In his official *Life* of his discovery Nicoll, writing for people with the bump of reverence highly developed, made no reference to this trait in his valuable friend. Instead, dealing with his subject's literary works, he launched on an essay on sentimentality, which is a masterpiece of special pleading, at once justifying Watson's practice and indicating his own complete awareness (for Nicoll was no fool in fundamental matters) of its vulnerability. A typical passage runs:

> " It is a fair question, 'Have we true pictures in these idylls? Is it thus and thus that people act or ever acted in a Scotch parish?' It must be remembered that idylls do not pretend to give a full chronicle of life. They try to seize the moments at which the hidden beauty of the soul leaps into vision. They do not take in the whole circumference of truth, and they do not profess to take it in. But they include a far wider area than is ever compassed by cynicism."

The repetition of that last word, even after an interval of twenty years, has a sinister ring in the context. But Nicoll must blunder on; there is no other word for it:

> " Anyhow, no one can possibly attach less importance to his books than the author did himself. . . . The fact is that he looked upon literature as a mere diversion from the actual work of his life, and did not consent either to stand or to fall by it."

This would be all very well, but Nicoll has already confused us by quoting with approval on a previous page Watson's own account of his difficulties with his early stories:

> " Each one was turned over in my mind for months before I put pen to paper. It took a prodigious amount of labour before I

even had a story formed in my head. Then I blocked it out at one sitting. Then the thing was put aside while I went over and over in my mind each detail, each line of dialogue, each touch of description, determining on the proper place, attitude, shape, colour and quality of each bit, so that the whole might in the end be a unit, and not a bundle of parts. By and by came the actual writing with the revision and the correction which accompanies and follows. The actual composition of the *Brier Bush* occupied fifteen months. They were the more difficult because in every case the character is revealed in dialogue exclusively. It is different when the writer has a plot. . . . "

It is almost as if the stylistic agonies of Flaubert, Pater and Henry James rolled in one went to the making of a short and simple book. Accepting Watson's own version of his travails as a creative writer, however, we may note the importance he put upon the use of dialect. This supports the theory that his cunning use of dialect in all its " quaintness " was a large factor in his commercial success. His account of his mountainous labours to produce moles also suggests, what I happen to believe to be the truth of the matter, that Watson was not a natural writer at all.

It would be a waste of time to analyse *Beside the Bonnie Brier Bush* and its successors in the same *genre*. These sketches are entirely based on long dialect passages in which the Scots farmer and villager are displayed as masters of a sort of dialectic in the Doric: wise, shrewd, pawky, intolerant of pretence, respectful above all of the Kirk and its authority, great sermon-tasters. So far as dialect and dialogue are interesting, this is able enough work, often amusing. But the connecting passages of narrative and of scenic description are flat. The deathbed theme recurs, indicating a poverty of invention. They are no more than anecdotes, aurally conceived.

John Watson, the modern world would say with complete justice, simply could not write ; and it is incredible that he was infinitely more successful in the commercial sense than others of the school who, not in the least afraid of laying the sentiment on with a trowel, had much more literary address. We can only conclude that his triumph was a freak of the circumstances already indicated.

The name of "Ian Maclaren" was on the title-page of eleven volumes published between 1894 and 1908. Most were in the *Brier Bush* class, but in *Young Barbarians* (1901) he did succeed in making a partial escape from the Free Kirk manse and in writing quite a breezy chronicle, presumably based on his own experiences at Perth Academy and Stirling High School, of the ways of Scottish schoolboys; and it is still a good enough book about boys—for boys. A posthumously published novel, *Graham of Claverhouse*, demonstrated that Watson, though a sound historian and in earnest as a novelist, had not the sort of mind—or perhaps he lacked the time for contemplation—to master the technique of narrative at length. It is an odd thing about *Graham of Claverhouse* that the dialogue in dialect, which was the foundation of his early popularity, is sparse. His gift was entirely for the anecdotal.

Watson died untimely, almost certainly of overwork; and again we face the recurrent paradox of his double career. The busy and devoted pastor of Sefton Park, the good citizen of Liverpool, found time to embark on three lecture tours in the United States. The first was the direct outcome of the huge and significant success of his *Brier Bush* tales in English-speaking America. It was made in the autumn of 1896 under the direction of that almost legendary organizer and bear-leader, Major J. B. Pond. We learn with astonishment that during the seventy-seven days between October 1 and December 16 Watson fulfilled ninety-six engagements. He lectured; he gave readings from his book; he preached as occasion required.

The success was undoubted. As Robertson Nicoll suggests, it was probably the greatest of any visiting lecturer since the days of Charles Dickens. Counting up his blessings in a remarkable volume entitled *Eccentricities of Genius*, Major Pond lusciously recalls the triumph:

> "He is a noble man. My heart is too full for utterance. Our tour has been a great success. In ten weeks we have cleared $35,795·91."

Ignoring the second point of decimals, we take it that Watson's efforts produced a profit—Pond specifically says "cleared"—of some £7,200. Even assuming that the lecturer's share was only one-half of this, but taking real values into account, we conclude that the minister of Sefton Park sailed from New York with, in his pocket, the contemporary equivalent of at least £10,000 for barely three months of very hard work.

He had entertained the guileless Americans with readings from his works, lectures on such subjects as "Traits of Scottish Humour" and sermons. The fabulous Major Pond offered him $24,000 if he would stay for another twelve weeks, but Watson had to refuse. He returned to the States, however, in 1899, again under the auspices of Pond, but details of neither the itinerary nor the profit and loss account are available now.

Having resigned from the charge of Sefton Park Church in 1906, he set out for the States once more in January, 1907, and it was his last earthly pilgrimage. He was overtaken by what was probably a streptococcal infection, affecting the throat and ears in the first place, and in the Brazelton Hotel, in Mount Pleasant, Iowa, far from Drumtochty, he died on May 6, 1907.

He was only fifty-seven. Probably he had tried to have it all ways since literary success fell upon him in a cascade in 1895 or thereabouts. He had few solid qualifications as a writer, but he was the exemplar of a considerable school of writing. He was otherwise a man of quite singular ability, apparently rather pompous in public, and we may well believe that he was a good and sincere man. Since we are concerned here mainly with literary values, we classify his case as one of the paradoxes of literature.

CHAPTER IV

IN a sense, however, the popularity of the Kailyard novelists during the last decade of the nineteenth century is a paradox from beginning to end. Even allowing for the influence of Robertson Nicoll and his *British Weekly*, it is hard to understand why just a few men closely connected with the Free Church of Scotland should have been the quite phenomenal " best-sellers " of a period. Some of the conditioning circumstances have already been suggested, but the more one studies the personal histories of the triumvirate—Barrie, Crockett and Watson—the more one is struck by the similarity of the circumstances in which they were nurtured.

It is perhaps little enough that all three were graduates of Edinburgh University; for Edinburgh had, and still has, the most numerous student body of all four Scottish universities, and the theological colleges were at hand. But is it not odd that two of them, Watson and Crockett, passed through New College into the ministry of the Free Church of Scotland, while Barrie, though no ecclesiastic, was also outside the pale of the Establishment? They all wrote in the first place of life as seen through the windows of the Free Kirk manse; they were all in some degree patronized by William Robertson Nicoll, a Free Churchman.

The non-Scottish reader must not be harassed by the niceties of denominationalism in Scotland, but the position of the Free Church in the nineteenth century must be understood. It was the outcome of a sensational split in the Established Church of Scotland in 1843 when, in the great

Disruption on the issue of the Kirk's relationship with the State, a considerable body of ministers—474 out of 1203—" walked out " of the General Assembly of the national Kirk and solemnly formed the new Free Kirk.

In the nature of things, the Free Kirk included the more liberal-minded sort of Scottish minister; they took away from the Establishment many of its ablest and most cultured forces. It lacked funds, except in so far as its adherents could provide them by voluntary subscription; it lacked patronage of any kind. But it did build new churches, and it founded its own theological halls. If its differences from the Establishment were political rather than doctrinal, its liberalism was one set up against a conservatism; and that liberalism extended to culture as well as to the ideal of religious freedom. It does not matter now that the Free Kirk, like Barrie's Auld Licht Kirk, is largely gathered into the *kraal* of a Church of Scotland on the defensive, with a sour rump of " Wee Free's " left behind in the outposts. We note simply that the men who marched in solemn procession through the streets of Edinburgh on May 18, 1843, to create a new Church on credit, as it were, bore in themselves the seed of a vast amount of talent, duly to be nurtured and to express itself in diverse ways. These Free Kirk manses, frugal, studious, earnest in well-doing, contributed to the more useful sort of British life during the second half of the nineteenth century a stream of able men out of all proportion to their number.

Samuel Rutherford Crockett might seem to have made a poor beginning in life. He was what is politely called the natural son of a Galloway farmer, born in the farmhouse of Little Duchrae in the very lovely country between Loch Ken and Kirkcudbright. That was in 1860, so that he and Barrie were of the same vintage year. The irregularity of his introduction to society does not appear to have affected the boy in any way. (The rate of illegitimacy in rural Galloway is always apt to be high.) He is described as being a lively lad when he went to school in Castle-Douglas ; he was clever enough to win a bursary at Edinburgh University, proceeding thither at the age of sixteen. The bursary was for only £20 a year, however, and young Crockett took to what is nowadays called freelance journalism to keep himself going. He was still a student when he contrived to acquire journalistic experience in London. Travelling as a tutor, he saw a good deal of Europe by the time he had come of age and profited by a semester at Heidelberg. He entered the Free Church of Scotland's New College in 1882 and left it in 1886, licensed to preach. In the latter year he became Free Kirk minister at Penicuik, in Midlothian, under the Pentland Hills and within ten miles of Edinburgh.

There is no official biography of Samuel Rutherford Crockett. Even Robertson Nicoll was not moved to improve the shining hour. Crockett had deserted the Free Kirk long before his death, and his popularity had sadly deserted him. Even so, we get from the fragments of reminiscence the impression of a lively and attractive personality. From his books we gather that he was what the Rev. Dr. John Watson never was—a natural writer. Not a great writer by a long chalk, but a writer considerably more competent within a limited range than some of his more successful contemporaries. Perhaps his mistake was to seek to extend that range beyond his capacities and so to fall between stools. As we shall see, Crockett was perhaps fatally torn between the appeals of the two contemporary inclinations of Scottish fiction—the romantic in the Scott-Stevenson tradition and the parochial in that of Barrie and Watson.

It appears that Crockett was a faithful and popular minister to the Free Kirk folk of Penicuik, but much of his heart was still in writing. Like Robertson Nicoll before him he contributed to the *Christian Leader*, and by 1893 he had a sufficiency of tales and sketches on hand to make a book, his first, *The Stickit Minister*. (A " stickit " minister is one who, having taken his classes and been duly licensed to preach, fails to find a charge.) This was quite an attractive collection, displaying along with several weaknesses some distinct potentialities. If anything, the stories lacked bite; their author could rarely face the relentless conclusion of his premisses; as with everything of the Kailyard School, they are about life as seen through the manse window. Even so, any contemporary critic worth his salt would have discerned talent behind the prentice hand. There was a roughish country freshness about some of the tales; this writer had a good eye for the elements of the Galloway scene.

The year of grace 1894 was Crockett's *annus mirabilis*. He was a prolific scribe, a good deal of a hack in his latter days, and he had ready for the press two novels in two different *genres*. One was pure Kailyard, *The Lilac Sunbonnet*; the other was Stevensonian romance with a bit of Kailyard thrown in, *The Raiders*. Both were immensely successful, if not quite sufficiently so to take Samuel Rutherford Crockett across the Atlantic into the arms of Major J. B. Pond. There was even a third novel that year, but it is completely forgotten.

The success was, however, enough to persuade the Free Kirk minister of Penicuik into resigning his charge and accepting the attractive but alarming hazards of the independent literary life. The decision was quite momentous in the period. It was a serious matter when an ordained Free

Kirk man exchanged the cure of souls for dalliance with the Muses. The affair was much discussed, with many shakings of the head, but Robertson Nicoll, always capable of getting down to brass tacks, talked sense in a letter to the inevitable Dr. Marcus Dods:

> " Crockett did right to resign, whatever happens. When he felt his main interest elsewhere it was not for his soul's health to keep a pastorate. What he will do and where he will turn ' being let go ' is a serious problem; but I hope for the best."

That was a judgment of great shrewdness. Poor Crockett did not succeed in going anywhere in particular. His popularity quickly deserted him, and his struggles to recover it were feverish and painful.

Of the two novels that made his name *The Raiders* is by far the better. It still circulates from public libraries in Scotland, at least, if only to juveniles, whereas *The Lilac Sunbonnet* is nearly forgotten.

The former is one of those numerous novels of romantic adventure that might never have been written had Stevenson not laid down the formula in *Kidnapped*. The first two sentences give the game away to the knowing reader.

> " It was upon Rathan Head that I first heard their bridle-reins jingling clear. It was ever my custom to walk in the full of the moon at all times of the year. . . . "

The manner, in short, is that of the *pastiche*, and we may admit that it is well sustained from first to last. The hero, inevitably, is strong and simple but dumb, the heroine —" May Mischief " in this case—subtle, mocking and beautiful. Their lot is to have their private affair confused with a smuggling episode on the Solway coast; they owe much to a wise, whimsical gipsy, Silver Sand (Alan Breck in a previous literary existence), and after many exciting adventures by flood and field they are duly in each other's arms.

The design is indeed familiar, but Crockett did apply to it some good qualities of his own. He displayed a sufficient capacity for invention and the creation of suspense. He had his own quite individual ear for the Galloway speech, his own excellent eye for the varied, beautiful and still insufficiently appreciated Galloway scene: the latter a capacity that was to stand him in better stead than Highland sunsets in the case of William Black. He also displayed even in this romance a purely personal quality which shocked the primmer critics of the period: a boisterous humour that was ever in danger of tumbling into crudity. This was no doubt the proper inheritance of the natural son of a small farmer; the Free Kirk minister had always been a lively lad.

The Lilac Sunbonnet is another kettle of fish altogether. For the stormy life of the Solway coast in the eighteenth century exchange the placid rural existence of nineteenth-century Galloway, a region of green fields and quiet villages. There are neither smugglers nor gipsies about in this world, but an appropriate sprinkling of grave elders and sharp-tongued old wifies. But if the setting is different, the atmosphere wholly domestic, the course of true love less complicated by physical danger, mists and moss-hags, the essential pattern of *The Raiders* is reproduced—the bone-headed but honest hero led by the wisdom and courage of an arch heroine to find peace and happiness at length in her arms. In this case the hero is a student of the theology of a small, narrow Presbyterian denomination; the heroine, always to be seen on fine days in a lilac sun-bonnet, is a farm lass with the Christian name of—believe it or not—Winsome.

It is hard for any reasonably literate adult of the mid-twentieth century to read *The Lilac Sunbonnet* without nausea. Despite Crockett's high spirits, despite his undoubted ability to keep a story moving, despite his fine feeling for the regional scene, one is revolted by that inveterate coarseness of which the better contemporary critics complained. This was not a coarseness in the moral sense; it was in his approach to character or scene, so that he seems capable of only the crudest psychology and will most blatantly man-handle probability in order to arrive at the right sentimental conclusion. Whether that sort of trimming was a necessity of the man's own spirit or his calculated notion of what his readers would require, it is now fruitless to inquire. We may forgive the technical crudity that can start a paragraph with "All this goes to introduce Meg Kessock . . ." and then proceed to describe the lady's history and place in society, but we hesitate over the chapter headings, which are, after all, the fruits of deliberation, and con such captions as "Curled Eyelashes," "The Love-Song of the Mavis," "Such Sweet Sorrow" and "The Dew of their Youth" with distaste. This is an arbitrary arrangement of life, apparently wilful.

The first few chapters of the tale are *pour rire* in our latter-day understanding. Ralph Peden, the divinity student now on holiday in Galloway, is studying his books by the side of Grannoch Water. He becomes aware, between moments of intense application to the Greek Lexicon and his notes, that two females are washing blankets in the stream, their skirts kilted high, their limbs exposed. In the description of the physical scene there is much of the mechanical. The stream "wimples," the glen is "drenched in sunshine." When Ralph Peden's eye at length focuses on the physical charms of Winsome Charteris, Crockett can find it possible to overwrite grossly:

"Fair hair, crisping and tendrilling over her brow, swept back in loose and flossy circlets till caught close behind her head by a tiny ribbon of blue—then again, escaping, it went scattering and wavering over her shoulders, wonderingly, like nothing on earth but Winsome Charteris's hair."

This absurd excess is repeated in his use of dialect. Her grandmother addresses Winsome:

" ' 'Deed, I'm no sae unbonny yet, for a' yer helicat flichtmafleaters, sprigget goons, an' laylac bonnets.' "

Again, in a nostalgic anecdote:

" ' . . . But they got an unco begunk. Ye see, my faither had bocht an awfu' thrawn young bull at the Dumfries fair, and he had been gaun gilravagin' aboot; an' whaur should the contrary beast betak' himsel' but to the Roman Camp on Craig Ronald, where the big ditch used to be? . . . He ran at Jock Hinderlands afore he could climb up a tree; an', fegs, he gaed up a tree withoot clim'in', I'se warrant, an' there he hung, hanket by the waistband o' his breeks, baa-haain' for his minnie to come and lift him doon, an' him as muckle a clampersome hobbledehoy as ever ye saw! ' "

The bewildered Englishman may be assured that even the Scottish reader with an interest in the old tongue finds these passages just a little bit too deliberately elaborate. Crockett provided his readers with explanations in footnotes, and his publishers added a glossary that covers seven pages in a double-column setting. This seems to emphasize the point already made: that contemporary interest in the Kailyard novels was rooted in part in the " quaintness " of dialect speech. On the evidence provided by *The Lilac Sunbonnet* it looks as if Crockett ploughed this field with deliberate assiduity.

One hesitates to extend the story of Crockett's " best-seller." Bemused by the sight of female beauty and naked legs, the divinity student hurries away, leaving his books behind. Arrived at the manse where he is staying with the Reverend Gilbert Welsh, he is catechized by that divine on his recent study of the last chapter of Proverbs. The views of King Lemuel's mother as to female virtue are supported by chapter and verse; the student has it all pat. Then

> " 'And what,' said the minister tentatively, leaning forward to look into the open face of the young man—'what is the distinction or badge of true beauty and favour of countenance, as it is so well expressed by the mother of King Lemuel?'
>
> " 'A LILAC SUNBONNET!' said Ralph Peden, student in divinity."

The reader should understand that Ralph has not so far made the lady's acquaintance, and it is really monstrous that Crockett should invite us to believe in a sudden infatuation, powerful enough to produce such a reply in the given circumstances. This is a case of the nearly impossible, the flagrantly arbitrary arrangement of fact to meet the need for prettiness. The tale is managed from beginning to end in such terms.

In the meantime, the incredible Winsome has observed the flight of the student and duly moves up the hillside to discover the books left behind in his prim confusion. She has already scented a potential sweetheart—and indeed indulges in some highly whimsical speculations as to his nature—and she removes the volumes with the idea of "planting" them next day when, as she justly surmises, he will return to retrieve them.

The inevitable meeting takes place according to Crockett's relentless programme, but the lady has meanwhile concealed his notebook in her bosom. They must together search for the missing item, and the details of the quest are best described in the slang of the years between the German Wars as being wholly "sick-making," with

> " . . . the two set to seeking, both bareheaded brown-cropped head and golden wilderness of tresses not far from one another, while the 'book of manuscript notes' rose and fell to the quickened heart-beating of that wicked and deceitful girl, Winsome Charteris."

The reader will not require to be assured that, while the course of such true love could not be wholly smooth, the affair duly ends in a rather more perfect happiness than most individuals find in this vale of tears.

One is tempted to say that *The Lilac Sunbonnet* is too gloriously bad to be true, even more fantastic than the works of Amanda McKittrick Ros, in that Crockett's jaunty air of realism conveys the impression that he really believed this mass of sludge to be pretty good and almost possible. But we have, again, no means of examining the conscience of any writer. Perhaps the man deluded himself. The massive and ineluctable fact remains that, for the reading public of 1894, this confection was wholly good and covetable.

It was Crockett's fate never to repeat his first, early successes. No doubt he maintained his commercial position with ease over a considerable period after 1894, but it is significant that he tended latterly to turn away from the Kailyard and stick to adventure in the heather or in foreign lands and fruity historical periods. He made a fair and popular pass at exploring a new field in *Cleg Kelly*, the story of an Edinburgh slum child, but it was vitiated as a social study by his besetting sentimentality. Some further tales of old-time adventure in Galloway—*Men of the Moss Hags* and *The Grey Man*, for instance—are still readable, but these were written on the tide of popularity aroused by *The Raiders*; and we see the talent of Samuel Rutherford Crockett dwindling into the production, at frequent intervals, of fustian tales with such titles as *Me and Myn* and *Bloom of the Heather*. Whether he had rapidly exhausted a small field or failed for some personal reason there is now insufficient evidence to tell.

My own analysis of the decline, for such it certainly was, would be under three heads—as a good Free Kirk preacher might say. Crockett as a novelist lacked a fixed point of direction; he dithered between the Kailyard and the Heather and so fell between stools. This makes the second point —that his talent, though often vivacious, was limited. My third point would be simply that he had the bad luck to be born heir to certain traditions that were shortly to be outworn. The experience of the South African War, the advent of the internal combustion engine, wireless telegraphy, the New Woman, and all other manner of strange things brought it about that even the least intelligent strata of the reading public in Great Britain and the United States were no longer interested in either the grudging cracks of pawky Scots elders round the parish pump or the heroic doings of eighteenth-century yeomen with Solway smugglers. The Scots writer of the period who lacked the power of adaptability was fated to be far behind the fair. However honest and capable Crockett was as an artificer of words, he must rest in the pillory with the others for failing, or refusing, to see (the case of *Cleg Kelly* taken into account) what was really happening in the world about him. There were probably too many old books and ideas lying about in those Free Kirk manses, too few new ones—and a wonderful faith that, in spite of all the signs, the Kirk's hegemony was really not about to collapse.

It is only fair to see a novelist like Crockett as one born in an unlucky hour. The Kailyard novel was a late flower of the Presbyterian predominance in Scottish life; that and memories of the Jacobites were shortly to prove unacceptable to twentieth-century citizens. No writer of unusual talent could continue to work in these terms, and the writer of insufficient talent must continue to deal in outmoded stuff. Barrie was in the former class and turned himself into the expert dramatist he was from the first obviously destined to be. Crockett, lacking that extra little bit of horse-power, could not create a bridge for himself and flogged himself, his talent and his material into the limbo.

Nothing, I think, better illustrates Crockett's status as a hangover from another era than the tone of the letters written to him by Stevenson from Samoa. These letters of the last two years at Vailima are painfully soaked in nostalgia. This is most marked in the long epistles to Barrie, urging that brilliant young man, obviously with hope, to undertake the long journey to the Pacific and talk to the dying exile about home. Crockett's feeling for the Lowland scene, along with his obvious debt to the greater man, deeply touched the sad heart of him who was sick for home; and Crockett's dedication to him of *The Stickit Minister* provoked one of the best of Stevenson's poems, beginning

"Blows the wind to-day, and the sun and the rain are flying. . . ."

It was something to have inspired a much greater writer to that confession of homesickness; and it is pleasant to know that a few of Crockett's tales of adventure are still in demand.

CHAPTER V

ON a sunny, fresh day of June, 1937, I drove across Scotland in order to witness, and subsequently to report for the B.B.C., the funeral at Kirriemuir of James Matthew Barrie. The newspapers had made much of the importance of the event, and my mind was adjusted to the ideas of a large, milling but hushed crowd of spectators, a grandly sombre procession of the mourning great, and the note of high solemnity in general.

Sure enough, as the car approached the Angus townlet, cocked up on a hill like a miniature Bridgnorth, it was apparent that the County Police had been drafted to the district in strength to deal with abnormally heavy traffic, and one had the feeling of occasion the experienced reporter knows so well. Within the little town itself, however, there was no more stir, perhaps rather less, than one would have expected to see on any market day. The most active persons in Kirriemuir that afternoon were the newsreel men, setting up their apparatus at points of vantage. An hotel bar was entirely in the occupation of newspaper men, one and all grumbling at having been dispatched to this outlandish spot on what was now unanimously regarded as " a dud story." Seeking to ascertain something of local opinion on the day's great event, all I could get out of the potman was a grunted " Barrie? Him! Not a hundred per cent, not a hundred per cent."

The precise meaning of this strange phrase was not at once clear to me but, making my way to the square which covers almost all the whole metropolitan area of Kirriemuir, I was astonished to see that the pavements were only thinly lined; one could pick and choose a position on the kerb anywhere. I found myself beside a gamekeeper, a netted bag over his shoulder and a 12-bore gun under his arm. He questioned me earnestly:

"Is it a funeral?"

And when I had explained the provenance of all these excitements, he lingered uneasily for five minutes or so and then turned away down a side street, the decision implying the depth of regional feeling about a matter of which the London newspapers had made so much. There flitted across my mind the notion that this unregarded return of the native would have been a good subject for one of the *Auld Licht Idylls*.

The funeral procession came, passed and disappeared. The small oaken coffin looked singularly grandiose within the country hearse. The procession of mourners behind was on foot. One observed the imperious features and moustache of Ramsay MacDonald, the kilt of Sir Harry Lauder. These and other important mourners were followed by the Provost and Town Councillors of Kirriemuir in their best blacks. The Principal of Edinburgh University and the President of its Students' Representative Council seemed to intrude on the dullness of the proceedings with the red, scarlet, yellow and purple of their gowns and hoods. For the rest, it might have been the funeral of a country doctor or the respected vice-convener of a county council. However solemn and moving the memorial service in St. Paul's, the burial procession behind the corpse of James Matthew Barrie, in his native town, was a shabby sort of affair. The man whose plays had filled the theatres of the world went drably to the grave to lie at length beside his mother.

My car had been left in a garage for a minor repair, and it was clear that there had been no knocking off work for the great local event. (I am sorry that this should contradict Mr. Denis Mackail's official account, but facts are facts.) To the foreman I expressed my genuine surprise that the funeral had seemed so unimpressive and popular interest in it so small.

"Barrie!" cried the foreman with passion. "Nobody round about here thought muckle of him!"

It is a Scottish weakness to be sourly jealous of success. The prophet has no great honour in that country. But I still think I heard in that mechanic's tones the note of a positive hostility, a genuine resentment. Taken with the bartender's mysterious remark, it seemed to complete a view commonly held among the ordinary folk of Kirriemuir that Barrie was not a true native of the place, and that in his works he had held them, or their fathers, up to ridicule.

It is true, as we shall shortly see, that Barrie's sojourn in the townlet he called Thrums was spasmodic, and no doubt the garage foreman could hardly be expected to know that the deepest impressions are acquired in early childhood, when the eye of the clever boy is sharp and the tablets of his mind are clean and sensitive. No reader of Barrie's earlier fiction, however, can escape the painful sense of being privy to an exposure. Whether or not *Margaret Ogilvy* amounts to a positive act of indecency is still a proper subject of debate. Here we must take the detached line and see that the Barrie trick of holding out his characters at arm's length, as it were, and making them perform their antics to our sardonic, even sadistic, delight was an early symptom of his instinctive sense of theatre. He seemed never to have lived with and among real people; everybody else was a marionette, floodlit but capable of the most amusing antics. He saw himself in the same light, to be sure.

He was wilful even in his handling of dialect, and one wonders if his long absences from the scene of his early tales had dulled his ear to the nuances of the Angus speech. I have known natives of that province, otherwise his worshipping admirers, who could lash themselves into fury over a locution he continually put into the mouths of his characters—" I sepad " he insisted on spelling it. Now this is simply his own phonetics for " I'se uphaud "; that is, " I would uphold," or as an Englishman would say in argument, " I maintain." It is indeed an awkward and arbitrary version of the original; something like a sneer in itself, something of a deliberate caricature. One could uphold the proposition that any man with a proper sense of language would have been content with the conventional rendering, " I'se uphaud." Or had Barrie been too long away from Kirriemuir, and too young when it first impressed him, to understand what the amphibrach truly represented in ordinary English speech?

We note merely that, in the period of Barrie's success as a novelist, the rendering of dialect was less systematized by common agreement than it is to-day. To this day the user of Scots in fiction (or poetry, for that matter) must make his own rules, even if the younger Scottish poets are bent on systematizing what they call " Lallans "—that is, the old Scottish language of the Lowlands. A very beautiful and supple language it is, if it may seem a thought late in the day to seek the artificial revival of something which long ago died a quite natural death. So far as the Kailyard men are concerned, meanwhile, the phoneticians could have quite a lot of fun comparing the renderings by Barrie, Watson and Crockett respectively of nearly identical phrases.

When all that is said and done, in James Matthew Barrie we are dealing with a writer who could have written ten Crocketts and twenty Ian Maclarens into a cocked hat at any moment. We consider now the case of a greatly gifted man, at least a near-genius, who was yet crude enough in his early years virtually to found the Kailyard School and, as a consequence, have all sorts of fourth-raters climbing by his bootstraps. It was Barrie and Robertson Nicoll in conjunction who brought off this fantastic triumph of sentimentality over British and American taste in a complacent age.

James Matthew Barrie was born in the weaving town of Kirriemuir, Angus, on May 9, 1860, being thus senior to Samuel Rutherford Crockett by only a few months. He was the ninth child and third son of David Barrie, a hand-loom weaver, and Margaret Ogilvy, a stonemason's daughter. The father was more than the average weaver, working alone in a room of his cottage; he employed others of his trade, and when the menace of the power-loom became inescapable, he took a responsible post with one of the new, large firms. J. M. Barrie was thus not born into poverty. Nor was he born into the narrow Auld Licht Kirk, for according to the custom of the time Margaret Ogilvy entered her husband's communion, and their children were brought up—mark the recurrent note!—in the Free Kirk. As we may guess, and as Mr. Denis Mackail explicitly states in his irritatingly arch but sensitive and well-informed biography, *The Story of J. M. B.* (Peter Davies, 1941), Barrie owed to his mother's reminiscences much of the material he used in his sketches of the communion to which she had belonged as a child. He really wrote in the first place of Kirriemuir as it was in 1840 or thereabouts. The use of the first person deluded the innocent Sassenach into believing that all this was a report on current conditions.

Two circumstances combined to give the boy an unusual sort of upbringing. His older brother had graduated at Aberdeen with First Class Honours in 1862 and in 1867 was appointed classical master in Glasgow Academy. The little house in Kirriemuir was crowded, and it was deemed right and natural that young Jamie should go to live in Glasgow with A. O. Barrie and the sister who was to keep house for him, and attend the famous school in which his brother taught. He had thus the unusual experience of living in a great industrial city for the best part of two years, between 1868 and 1870, and of getting his schooling in what is nowadays called a secondary school.

A change in the family fortunes brought this period to an end in the summer of 1870. Then David Barrie accepted a post in the sizable town of Forfar, and A. O. Barrie left Glasgow Academy. Young James returned to the family circle and attended Forfar Academy for the best part of two years. Then the Barries were back again in Kirriemuir and the boy was eventually sent to the local Free Church school. Then again the indefatigable A. O. Barrie was appointed to the inspectorate of schools and given a south-western district to look after, with headquarters in Dumfries, and he repeated the suggestion that Jamie should come once more to stay with him and the housekeeping sister and attend Dumfries Academy, another excellent secondary school of the grammar school type. So the boy went to Dumfries Academy in the autumn of 1873 and remained a pupil there until he had finished his schooling five years later.

One might think all this very unsettling for a clever and sensitive youngster, but there is Mr. Mackail's word for it that these were perhaps the happiest five years of Barrie's life. He was a lively boy, eager for country adventure, walking and fishing and talking. He read voraciously, according to type, scribbled much and did well in his classes. He was a leading light of the school debating society, and the then Rector of Dumfries Academy must have been a remarkable man of his period in countenancing the participation of his senior pupils in a local dramatic group, of which the existence stirred young Barrie to some extraordinary projects, at least.

It is wrong, however, to think that this was exile from Kirriemuir, and that his life there ended at the age of seven. All the long school holidays were spent with his own people in Angus; Kirriemuir remained his base until he finally, at the age of twenty-four, embarked for London and the siege of Fleet Street. At the same time, it is permissible, and useful, to surmise that the boy's long absences from home during the formative years encouraged his instinct to see Kirriemuir and its people through opera glasses, as it were. He was so far *déraciné*.

Indeed, this phase of the man's life has been explained at some length only because the circumstances of Barrie's boyhood were immensely different from those of the average Scots lad of his position and period. The long terms of absence from the essential family circle must have had their effect, however subtle, on a boy so sensitive and precocious. The separation of any child from any mother still alive has its implications; and the perceptive reader will appreciate that Barrie's situation was not at all that of a child sent to boarding school according to family custom in the English mode. In fact, the arrangement was all against the run of Scottish tradition; and we may fairly wonder if his experience of schooling, in days of indifferent communications, did not intensify the "mother fixation" which was, quite clearly, a large part of his psychological make-up. He was always something of the lost child and was apt in his maturity and old age to dramatize the part. The theme runs clear through most of his works from *Sentimental Tommy* to *Peter Pan*, from *When a Man's Single* to *The Old Lady Shows her Medals*.

Mr. Denis Mackail has fully and shrewdly analysed all this in his biography, and we have no concern here with the "character" Barrie ultimately made of himself, when he became the intimate of the great in the land, nor indeed with anything but his Kailyard phase and the circumstances that more obviously conditioned his writings in that kind. The period between 1878 and 1884 included studies at Edinburgh University and an M.A. degree—three years; a surprising appointment as leader writer with the *Nottingham Journal*—two years; intense activity as a freelance journalist and the ultimate descent upon London—one year. (He was so poor and shy on his arrival that he carried his own trunk, or box, down the whole length of the platform at St. Pancras.) The work of the next ten years is our chief concern here.

Thousands of gifted young Scots, the cheaply-hired, reliable D.P.'s of the newspaper industry, have reached London in similar circumstances, but few went into the fray so well-equipped in the given journalistic circumstances as James Matthew Barrie. We must try to envisage a newspaper world then still far from trustification, still unclouded by the fetish of "news value" that has so dangerously elevated the mere eavesdropper and relegated the real writer in the scale of Press values. There were more and better newspapers in those days; fewer "executives" and more editors with real editorial authority; smaller circulations and higher standards of real writing.

The great editors of the day cared for writing as such without reference to its topicality. There was none of that subtle pressure from the big advertiser which (though modern newspaper proprietors hotly deny its existence) tends to force the intellectual level of the contemporary sheet down to that of the lowest common denominator—in effect, that of the largest mass of uncritical and easily impressed citizens, the potential buyers of advertised goods. There was always room for " a bit of good writing," and those bits of good writing had as much validity within the journalistic scheme of those happy days as what is nowadays called a big story. (Mr. Mackail tells how young Barrie, arriving in London, saw the title of one of his articles on a placard in the station while he was still wrestling with his box.) Editors were pleased to print sketches long enough to be called short stories.

One of the great editors of the period was Frederick Greenwood, of the *St. James's Gazette*, an autocrat and a magnificent discoverer and nourisher of talent. He and Barrie had already discovered each other, and it was to Greenwood's address that the latter now mainly devoted himself—mainly but not by any means entirely. The fertility of ideas in this young Scot was beyond belief; he could apparently write anything, at any time, for any sort of periodical, and usually succeed in getting it printed. He was quite ruthless as a freelance, in that he would cheerfully take a subject of which he knew absolutely nothing and still make a readable article out of it. Even his biographer is at a loss to account fully for his ramifying activities in the freelance field.

But Greenwood was still his most important target, and soon those whose business it is to look out for exploitable talent were taking heed of those recurrent articles in the *St. James's Gazette*, mostly on " quaint " Scottish subjects and all written in a highly individual and cunning manner. The wary Aberdonian eye of Robertson Nicoll did not fail to spot the future winner, and shortly Barrie was writing for the *British Weekly* those sketches which, with some published *sub regno* Greenwood, were to make up the *Auld Licht Idylls*. The book-publishing power of Messrs. Hodder & Stoughton did not fail to appeal to the ambitious little man from Kirriemuir—61 inches in height with slightly bow legs, a huge head and an immense amount of cleverness inside that notable feature.

Barrie's fecundity as a contributor to the newspapers and periodicals of his time is here dwelt on with deliberation. The modern student of the works of the Kailyard triumvirate is apt to be puzzled by the vast numbers of books they contrived to write and get published while the cabbage-patch was in good heart. Three in one year from one pen alone was not out of the ordinary. Then it is seen on investigation that the publishing circumstances of the period favoured this apparent luxuriance. Those were the days when the independent author could fairly reckon on the profitable serialization of a tale before its appearance in book form; when the publisher smiled more blandly than he does nowadays on volumes of "collected pieces." The Kailyard men flourished in the first place mainly on books made up and out of articles and sketches duly made over. (This accounts, of course, for the scrappy quality of most of the standard Kailyard books.) In an excellently perceptive passage Mr. Denis Mackail shows how Barrie seems to have expressed most of his leading notions in his early journalism, and how they keep recurring in the books and plays to the end of his long writing career.

With *Auld Licht Idylls* (1888), however, he introduced Thrums and the queer people of that small denomination to a highly appreciative public. It is a short book by modern standards, consisting of about a dozen sketches of varying lengths. The narrator is ostensibly the schoolmaster of Glen Quharity, a privileged and somewhat patronizing observer of life in neighbouring Thrums, and he vastly enjoys himself in holding up his marionettes to be laughed at; the applause of the gallery is invited. The Auld Licht folk are seen from without, usually as persons of glum countenance and bleak minds; very rarely is the attempt made to interpret them from within. When the tale is sad, on the other hand, the pathos is apt to be laid on with a trowel, and very little is sacred to this showman. It is perhaps the most puzzling thing about Barrie from first to last that the expert toucher of emotions, the weaver of charmingly whimsical webs, the delight of the nurseries, had in all his dealings as a writer with such topics as death and sepulture and grief and suffering the way of a sadist. Perhaps he tortured himself thus; but the morbid psychology of James Matthew Barrie is, fortunately, Mr. Denis Mackail's concern, not mine.

And then the stuff was so confoundedly readable, and is so to this day. The narrative is beautifully attractive in a clean, telling prose, the purely visual descriptions of the scene are admirable. Barrie could write wonderfully until his fatal facility (in these early books at least) for the improbable, the jest at any price, brings the sensitive reader up with a jerk. You get the unfortunate impression of a man writing below his own standards in order to achieve the quick, cheap effects; and that affronts the most tolerant critical faculty to-day. The Scottish reader has the unhappy feeling of being betrayed to make a Roman holiday. Scots people are legitimate figures of fun in certain aspects of their behaviour, relative to that of other races, but fun is only fair when it is sympathetic.

One thinks to perceive in Barrie's Kailyard writings either a positive dislike of his own people or a blatant desire to gratify the prejudices of other peoples. He very readily sold the pass.

This element in the work is pervasive, fundamental. We can catch young Barrie out in much cruder faults, even if they were the faults of inexperience: in exaggerations, in wholly false emphases, in deliberate twistings of probability to make an effective end. These twistings could never, with such an adroit handler of the pen, be so crude as Crockett's, but they are all the more venal in that Barrie must in his artistic conscience have known so much better.

One of the sketches is largely concerned with the ritual of christening within the Auld Licht communion. We are told that the custom was to have an infant brought into church for the first time within at least a fortnight of its birth; and the whole point of this anecdote is that, the wife of an elder of the kirk having given birth to a child at ten minutes before midnight on a Saturday, and the child being produced for baptism next morning, it was concluded (with the local gossips assisting) that the Sabbath must have been broken in order to prepare the infant for the ceremony. Barrie concludes the tale:

> "For the defence, Bell maintained that all preparations stopped when the clock struck twelve, and even hinted that the bairn had been born on Saturday afternoon. But Sandy knew that he and his had got a fall. In the forenoon of the following Sabbath the minister preached from the text, 'Be sure your sins will find you out'; and in the afternoon from 'Pride goeth before a fall.' He was grand. In the evening Sandy tendered his resignation of office, which was at once accepted. Wobs were behindhand for a week owing to the length of the prayers offered up for Bell; and Lang Tammas ruled in Sandy's stead."

This sort of guff might appeal to a Cockney commercial

traveller as a true picture of the sort of thing that could happen in Scotland, where they all wear the kilt and eat haggis, but most modern readers, one hopes, would throw the book across the room and cry: "I simply don't believe it!"

Young Barrie's lapses of judgment and taste are recurrent throughout the book, even in less onerous concerns than human behaviour. He simply could not play fair with his puppets; he was showing them off to his London patrons in their crude simplicity. Even the simplest dialect word must be within quotation marks, so that one is driven to believe that he was ashamed of his own Scottishness. Very readable and rather revolting—that would be a quite fair assessment of J. M. Barrie's first success to-day.

It is odd that Mr. Mackail, like Robertson Nicoll before him, is moved in the biography to discuss Barrie's choice of the lovely and wholly inappropriate word "Idylls." Thus:

> "Why? Because he thought it was a good title, because he thought these sketches of meanness and even brutality idyllic, or because he was being ironical? The first seems much the most likely; yet if we get him on cock-fighting or funerals there isn't a hint that he is less callous than what he describes. As for irony, it was always one of his tools or weapons; but again and again there is something much blunter and more openly offensive in the treatment of his fellow-townspeople. In this book he almost seems to grudge them their good qualities. No wonder they resented it and even hated it—until pride in his later successes made them forgive even this."

(One may doubt, on evidence already advanced, if that last clause is justified, but let Mr. Mackail continue.)

> "But in England and London it was the newness and freshness that stood out; the lifting of the lid from scenes and lives of which most readers knew nothing. Here the mockery was flattering, the fun completely innocent and harmless, and the formlessness no particular drawback in a book so entirely unlike anything else. A Scotch village would obviously be peopled by curious and ridiculous

characters, preoccupied with parsimony and religion. They recognized what they took to be the truth even more clearly, perhaps, than the strange quality of the author's workmanship and mind. They were amused and accepted him as a new humorist, with special Saxon relish in a Scotchman being a humorist at all."

As an analysis of the factors which made the Kailyard novels so enormously popular that last paragraph could hardly be bettered, and perhaps one should not ask Mr. Mackail, or Barrie's ghost, for a few words on the artist's obligation to respect absolute truth. In another part of the biography Mr. Mackail argues with conviction that Barrie's ruthlessness, his lack of regard for certain private sanctions, was the sign of the pure artist at work, but the theory hardly covers the man's exaggerations, improbabilities and sheer perversions of ascertainable fact. In all this early work Barrie was demonstrably a dishonest artist, as clever as a bagful of monkeys, but regardless of truth. He simply must get the sentimental, dramatic effect his temperament required, and that at any cost. He was probably saved from ultimate extinction by the discovery of his unique talent for the pretty illusions and arbitrary arrangements of the stage. He never even began to be a novelist by any detached critical standard. He was supremely good only over the relatively short distances of sketch or play.

The case of *The Little Minister* (1891) is much to this point. This amorphous, irritating and frequently enchanting work was to be " the big novel " of which every young writer dreams, to which the critics continually urge him. Barrie retired from London to Kirriemuir for a time to write it; it runs to some 150,000 words, still a long novel in this present day of a fashion for long novels. It could be docked of at least one-third of its content and thereby improved; it has so many technical faults, so many blatant crudities, one wonders that Barrie did not, in the affluence which subsequently came to him, suffer it to be quietly forgotten, for the sense of structure he learned on the stage to such excellent effect must surely have been exacerbated by this wambling and wholly improbable tale. Take away the " quaintness " of the Auld Licht environment, and the structure collapses. Written in 1950, one dares to think, it would certainly never be published as it stands.

It is all about a callow minister of the Auld Licht connection, Gavin Dishart by name, and the enchanting girl, Babbie, one of those clever, mischievous girls without whom no Kailyard hero could get anywhere. She is the ward of an earl, no less, Lord Rintoul, who proposes in his maturity to marry her. There is a riot of the weavers in Thrums, however; the military are called in, and the girl, dressed as a gipsy, enters the town and persuades the decorous young clergyman to go to the almost unimaginable length of throwing a clod of turf at one of the soldiers. Thus is set the inevitable situation—the temptation of the young man, the jealousy of Lord Rintoul (who is in the best tradition of melodrama), and the heavy disapproval of the Auld Licht elders of their minister's infatuation for " the Egyptian." A sort of gipsy marriage " over the tongs " comes into this farrago, and the situation thus created with the sour and oafish elders of young Dishart's kirk is such that his manse is in a state of " siege."

This hopeless—and utterly impossible—tangle is unravelled when, in a disastrous flood, the young minister is marooned on the River Quharity (the Clova in actuality), and above the roaring of the waters conducts for his elders on the safe bank a sort of burial service for himself, accompanied by a vocal recital of his last will and testament. Thus the gnarled, mean men decide that Gavin, duly rescued after nearly losing his life to save one of his flock, is a really good man and Babbie a fit *châtelaine* of the manse.

It is all too easy to ridicule a story by detailing its plot in plain words, but *The Little Minister* is in the coldest fact ridiculous; and that is to say nothing of its technical blemishes. (Mr. Mackail, to do him justice, deals with these faithfully.) A stage version was produced in due course, and the thing was extremely popular in both forms. It was serialized in *Good Words*, moreover; its success gave the earlier books a new lease of life; and at twenty-nine James Matthew Barrie was commercially successful to an extent quite unusual in his or any other generation.

Two contemporary opinions on *The Little Minister* help us to understand the temper of the period. First, Robertson Nicoll in a letter:

> "The Little Minister is wildly improbable, but is it not a rich book, with many pretty little things about it? There is much heart in it too. . . . "

though one may well hesitate over his odd pronouncement to Dr. Marcus Dods:

> "Barrie will succeed, and that soon. He is one of the men—more numerous, I fancy, than we think—who are every way improved by success—softened, humbled and redeemed from cynicism."

Then Stevenson wrote to the author direct, and the wise reader will bear in mind that writing to any novelist about his own work is a ticklish business:

> "Your descriptions of your dealings with Lord Rintoul are frightfully unconscientious. You should never write about anybody until you persuade yourself at least for the moment that you love him, above all anybody on whom the plot revolves. It will always make a hole in the book; and, if he has anything to do with the

> mechanism, prove a stick in the machinery. . . . *The Little Minister* ought to have ended badly; we all know it did; and we are infinitely grateful to you for the grace and good feeling with which you lied about it. If you had told the truth, I for one could never have forgiven you. As you had conceived and written the earlier parts, the truth about the end, though indisputably true to fact, would have been a lie, or what is worse, a discord in art. If you are going to make a book end badly, it must end badly from the beginning. . . . Now your book began to end well. You let yourself fall in love with, and fondle, and smile at your puppets. Once you had done that, your honour was committed—at the cost of truth to life you were bound to save them."

"At the cost of truth to life" is the operative phrase. R. L. S. phrased his lecture on a technical failure with wonderful grace, but we can fairly read into the passage his exasperation with the constructional defects of a young writer of so much promise. It will always be a puzzle that one of the most expert craftsmen the theatre has ever known was so ham-fisted over the long, slow stretches of fiction. But R. L. S. was speaking as the journeyman in the workshop, and the reading public of the period did not care at all for any of these professional demurrers. They were all for the sacrifice of "truth to life," delighted to have the universal inferiority complex soothed by Barrie's trick of deft narrative and quick, surprising flashes of perception, so like those of a clever woman. Mr. Mackail prefers to call it his "magic," and that is as may be. It was a magic that dodged an awful lot of truths which another sort of artist would have found ineluctable.

James Matthew Barrie cultivated the Kailyard assiduously for eight years on end, from 1888 until 1896. Then he turned to the more difficult problems of such a novel as *Sentimental Tommy*, which, though based geographically on Thrums, tackled the difficult problem of the artistic temperament. (Barrie never failed to be vastly interested in the miracle of his own talent. He had a childish and harmless delight in standing aside and marvelling that he should be such a clever little boy.) His commercial success during these eight years had been phenomenal. The publishers' advertisements on the end-pages of *Margaret Ogilvy* (1896) announce " The Thistle Edition "—the superb American Edition of J. M. Barrie's Novels, Tales and Sketches: eight volumes illustrated with photogravures by Hatherall and Bernard Partridge. This was limited in Britain to 500 copies at £3 15s. the set, and the rich could get one of 50 sets on hand-made paper, printed and bound by De Vinne, at ten guineas.

This was remarkably good going for a young man in his middle thirties; and the contemporary author must marvel that it was all done on slight collections of previously published material. It is safe to say that, conditions having changed so much, no publisher would to-day dare to offer to the public at the ruling prices books so short as those which made for Barrie a fortune as well as a reputation. *Margaret Ogilvy*, bought by the public in both Britain and the United States by the ten thousand, is rather less in total length than this brief study of the Kailyard School as a whole. This is not to denigrate Barrie's worth as a creative artist. It is, however, deliberately to suggest that any useful inquiry into the nature of his commercial triumph must take into account the level and condition of public taste at that period.

For the rest, it is necessary to cast at least a glance at two of the young man's later confections in the Kailyard tradition —*A Window in Thrums* and *Margaret Ogilvy*. These are " key " works; they almost seem to give the show away, the latter especially. The first was written—or, more correctly, assembled—in the early period, in 1889 to be exact. The second was produced in 1896, after the death of his mother.

On the face of it, *A Window in Thrums* is just such another collection of sketches as *Auld Licht Idylls*, in this case loosely bound together by the narrator's viewpoint from a weaver's tiny cottage on one of Kirriemuir's numerous hillocks. The protagonists are the penurious weaver, Hendry, his wife Jess, and his daughter Leeby. The two females, at least, see a great deal through their window, and whether he was aware of it or not, Barrie presents them as an intolerable couple of gossips and peeping Thomasinas. (On the whole, I think we must take it that Barrie was consciously guying his own people. He was incapable of pity for his fictional victims.) The rest is an aggregation of " sketches," and so far as the book has any plot, much is made towards the end of the return from London of a vagrant son, a barber in that city. He has brought home to Thrums a pledge of love—a glove; and a great deal is made of his mother's elaborate devices to persuade him eventually to put the thing on the fire in her presence. Then the faithful daughter Leeby dies in the convenient way of Victorian worthies; her husband obediently predeceases Jess by a measurable number of hours; and we are left eventually to weep over the return of the son, who has made a mess of things with the bad London girl whose glove he had carried, as he pays a valedictory visit to Thrums and quite incredibly bumbles over the scenes of his infant happiness.

Barrie's technical dexterity apart, this is sorry stuff in terms of life. Given the man's female gift of touching the springs of tears, it is a farrago, prefabricated; a debauch of sentimentality. At the same time, it is of great interest in relation to the book called *Margaret Ogilvy*, which (as we would say nowadays) really spills the beans.

The abortive adventure into the affairs of the Little

Minister apart, Barrie really wrote throughout his Kailyard period for, out and from his mother. The complex was more than maternal; it seems to have been positively foetal. Both Barrie himself in *Margaret Ogilvy* and Mr. Mackail in the official biography leave us in no doubt on this point.

Margaret Ogilvy (1896) carries on the title-page the frank confession—" by her son, J. M. Barrie." It is dedicated " To the Memory of my Sister, Jane Ann." And perhaps the acute reader has already guessed the identity of Margaret Ogilvy and Jane Ann Barrie with Jess and Leeby of *A Window in Thrums*.

One may very well wonder why *Margaret Ogilvy* was ever written, except for private circulation, but Barrie threw the portrait of his mother into the whirlpool of commerce: in cold fact, cashing in on his own popularity. Not many men would deliberately expose their own domestic affairs in this fashion, but Barrie was one of the few; and we can only conclude that commercial success, after a chilly boyhood, had turned his head. On the other hand, it is difficult to determine whether or not *Margaret Ogilvy* is true to the facts of the woman's life.

You never know where you are with Barrie. He could lie like a trooper to get the wanted, decisive effect; he made a world to suit his own fancy. For all his reputation for the understanding of women and children, we have to deal here with what seems to be a case of refined sadism. The modern reader may very well find that Margaret Ogilvy, on her son's evidence, is a distinctly self-centred old party, wearing out a faithful daughter (the Jane Ann of the dedication) to die before herself and assuming a vast amount of credit, if not responsibility, for her son's success in journalism and literature.

In one of his earliest books Barrie has a character who boasts that he " could write an article on my mother's coffin." In one of the more painful passages in *Margaret Ogilvy*, dealing with his mother's loss of a favourite son and with his own efforts to fill the emotional gap, he declares: " One does not ask a mother if she knows that there is a little coffin in the house." The reader of 1950, all too conversant with suffering, may conclude that the little man succeeded in both these enterprises.

That—like the indignation of the contemporary Scot against what he conceives to be a gross misrepresentation of his own people—is, however, a belated and perhaps topical judgment. We always come back to the stubborn fact that the Barrie tales were not only vastly popular with the general public in their day, but that his craftsmanship was lavishly praised by his peers. Writing as one highly conscious artist to another, Robert Louis Stevenson said in a letter to Henry James:

> " But Barrie is a beauty, the *Little Minister* and the *Window in Thrums*, eh? Stuff in that young man; but he must see and not be too funny. Genius in him, but there's a journalist at his elbow —there's the risk. Look, what a page is the glove business in the *Window* ! Knocks a man flat; that's guts if you please."

We could wish that R. L. S. had been spared to leave us his views on the propriety of *Margaret Ogilvy*, but it is much to the point that he had apparently no complaint against the matter of Barrie's early writings, excessively sentimental and positively false as so much of them now appear to us to be.

In another way of putting it: the Kailyard men are hardly worth discussing as practitioners of literature; we should really be addressing ourselves once more to a study of the social conditions and the state of the public mind that made their writings so immensely acceptable to the people of Great Britain and the United States of America in the last two decades of the nineteenth century.

CHAPTER VI

WE may therefore resume the argument by saying that the purely Scottish complaint against the betrayal of national dignity by the Kailyard writers is understandable but belated. It ignores certain historical factors, from which any detached student could easily judge that Scottish literature, however it may develop henceforward, was fated for a long time to be domestic, limited, parochial.

The violence of the Reformation in Scotland and the subsequent religious wars shattered the tradition of the Makars—Henryson, Dunbar and the rest—and set the nation back in every respect except pride and character. Whatever the modern apologists may say, the Calvinistic rule of life imposed by the Kirk over more than two centuries, as by a Gestapo, was fatal to artistic freedom and such luxuriance of creation as the English compromise of Episcopalianism allowed. A primitive economy favoured the dispersal of a population, never large, into remote groups, much obsessed by the ardours of winning a living from the soil. The national culture was of the rural kind, distinctly non-literary; and the removal of the native aristocracy to England in the train of James I of England and VI of Scotland removed, as we have already noted, the conventional resources of patronage.

The Scottish people, though feeling like a nation, though indeed acting as an independent nation until the cause was quite hopeless in the given circumstances, was thus and thus thwarted in its aesthetic development. The Kirk can be credited with the leadership of the continuing revolt against

English supremacy; but the really hideous paradox is that, in doing so, the Scottish churchmen, working to John Calvin's book of rules, quite blotted out from the vision of the folk such heady sights as the foam of perilous seas in faery lands forlorn. It is unpopular to-day, when the ministry of the Church of Scotland is ever so cultured, ever so forward-looking and open-minded, to suggest an unfortunate past, but at the bar of cultural history the Scots Kirk, in all its absurd and ramifying denominations, will find it hard to justify its way with the singers and the chaps who wanted to be jolly. It merely succeeded, really, in driving the Scots folk to hard drinking. . . . It is, by the way, an odd fact that Barrie rarely mentions this predominant *motif* of Scottish life. Perhaps he was frightened of what his mother might say.

The Scots therefore faced the impact of the Industrial Revolution with singularly few means of expressing themselves on that tremendous topic. The event hit Scotland with a resounding bang, with the real effect of a seismic disturbance, but not a word out of her representative writers! Robert Burns, who was much less of a fool than his idolators make him out to be, was a wholly countrified man, devoted, if a thought spasmodically, to "the fireside clime." The mighty genius of Walter Scott spent itself mainly on the baronial; and his magnificent flashes of contemporary observation were all in the rustic mood. There was a strange lack of literary talent in Scotland between 1830 and 1880; and R. L. Stevenson was a special case of the invalid-aesthete. In the last two decades of the nineteenth century there was simply nobody to report with reasonable fidelity on the state of Scotland. And it was precisely during this dark and difficult period that the Kailyard practitioners arose to sentimentalize and popularize a merely vestigial and completely unrepresentative Scotland.

We have already noted that the three prize blooms of the Kailyard were adherents—two of them in fact ordained ministers—of the Free Church of Scotland. It is as if that "liberal" and now nearly extinguished denomination had the literary business of Scotland under control. Actually, it was a case of a reasonably cultured and decidedly well-educated group cornering an easy market. Most able Scots of the period were busy making money in coal, iron, ships and textiles. Writing was a game for soft characters, unsuited to appearances in the bloody arena of commerce. You could leave it to the ministers—and the ministers were willing to write only of their small and comprehensible parishes, where man was vile enough but amusing and the manse was as the Palace of Westminster.

It is the sublime, almost farcical, paradox of the period that the Kirk, sitting pretty in its nineteenth-century hegemony, did not see, and certainly did not do anything about, the wholesale importation of Irish-Catholic labour in conditions that would nowadays seem rather shameful in our treatment of Displaced Persons. Thus the school population of Glasgow alone is about 30 per cent Roman Catholic and tending to increase as against the Presbyterian continence.

Such was the set of circumstances that favoured the emergence of the Kailyard School of novelists. Its success in England and in the States has already been adequately explained in the quotation from Mr. Denis Mackail's biography of Barrie on page 66.

On the purely literary side of things, we see the talented young Scotsman humbugged over at least two centuries of time by the rustic convention imposed, I seriously suggest, by the influence of the Kirk. The Kailyard inclination dates from long before Barrie, Crockett and the Reverend Dr. John Watson enjoyed its apotheosis.

Reference has already been made to the loose generalization that credits John Galt with the fatherhood of the Kailyard School. This is to misunderstand economic and social history. Galt did live into the early decades of the industrial era—and wrote indeed a preposterous but frequently amusing and historically interesting collection of tales called *The Steam-Boat*—but he was a child of eighteenth-century Ayrshire and wrote out of the sharp impressions of rural life acquired as a child in the period, 1780–90. He was too naturally humorous, too direct, too unpatronizing—too much the heaven-sent artist—to be lumped with the self-conscious exhibitors of the later development. John Galt may be criticized as a complete ass in his squandering of great talents on imitative and ill-digested themes, but I dare to assert the view that *The Annals of the Parish*, *The Entail* and *The Provost* will be cherished when even Barrie's very best is forgotten. Not one of the Kailyard triumvirate could have accomplished the bite and humour of that neglected masterpiece, *The Provost*. It was a singular pleasure for all literate Scots to find that excellent critic, Mr. V. S. Pritchett, saying a good and balanced word for old John in his admirable study of *The Living Novel*.

As J. H. Millar shrewdly pointed out, we get an early whiff of the Kailyard odour in—of all unexpected places—*Noctes Ambrosianae*. This is a surprising pointer indeed, but when the matter is examined we do see Wilson (or " Christopher North ") patronizing and exploiting the rustic ways of thought and speech, especially in the case of poor Hogg who, in his moments of inspiration, could write ten Wilsons off the map. Only pure genius could produce the like of *Bonny Kilmeny* or *The Memoirs of a Justified Sinner*. It was rather like making a superior sort of Edinburgh fun of Burns and his countrified ways, like listing that wild lad with the Kailyard men on the strength of that one sad and painful poem, *The Cottar's Saturday Night*. We may thank Providence that the dignity and decency of Walter Scott left us the best portrait of Burns in his maturity: the great poet seen as a true man through the eyes of a child of genius. What would we not give to have Shakespeare as seen through the eyes of, say, a young Milton!

An important agent in the process of decline which led to the fantastic success of the vestigial Kailyard-delvers was D. M. Moir (1798–1851), who contributed copiously to *Blackwood's Magazine* under the pseudonym of " Delta " and was in fact a practitioner of medicine in Musselburgh, an old fishing port that is now virtually a suburb of Edinburgh. He created, roundly and solidly enough, the figure of *Mansie Wauch*, " Tailor in Dalkeith," perhaps thereby inventing the device of the wise, pawky commentator and anecdotalist that has stood so many Scots writers in good stead over so many years. It may be said that *Mansie Wauch* is a good deal less offensive to native taste than most of the *fin-de-siècle* lucubrations. There is in it a good deal less nudging of the elbow, less playing to the gallery. One feels on the whole that Dr. Moir was writing with complete honesty about the things that pleased his simple soul. But one may think that he started a fashion that was to hinder Scottish literary development over a long period.

In favour of these older writers in this *genre*, however, it may be said that they were genuinely interested in the suppleness and variety of Doric speech. They rendered it in its fullness, without any canny regard for the taste of a metropolitan audience and without those self-conscious, apologetic quotation marks and footnotes that disfigure the pages of Crockett and Barrie.

A notable performer in this manner was William Alexander (1826–1894), for many years the editor of an Aberdeen newspaper and the author of *Johnny Gibb of Gushetneuk*. As has been remarked, this still vital work would completely baffle all but a few non-Scottish readers, and its author therefore escapes the charge of pandering that can be fairly laid against the triumvirate. It is in fact a pity that Alexander should ever have been lassooed into the Kailyard group by a careless classification; for while *Johnny Gibb* is admittedly scrappy and anecdotal in structure, it is in essence a serious study in rustic speech and as such of profound interest to philologists, who still delight in comparing Moir's handling of the Lothian dialect with Alexander's brilliant rendering of the Buchan variant.

But we are not concerned here to catalogue all those writers, mainly insignificant, who could or can be regarded as *alumni* of the School. Who but a few specialists, an occasional browser in antique circulating libraries, has in our time perused the works of Thomas Nicoll Hepburn, who, as "Gabriel Setoun," wrote quite respectably in the Kailyard mode in such tales as *Barncraig* and *Sunshine and Haar*? Who nowadays, though he is not so very long dead, considers the respectable works of Joseph Laing Waugh, creator of a popular figure called "Rabbie Doo"? The argument now is rather that what we call, loosely enough, the Kailyard strain is persistent in Scottish writing, however much the moderns may deplore the fact, and however gallantly they seek to shock their contemporaries out of their chronic addiction to gossip round the parish pump. We always return to the point that the Scots, for all their great civic and administrative, scientific and academic qualities, remain inveterately backward in literary culture—bewildered and sentimental children bleating for the old securities of the parochial life.

If this needs proving, consider the fact that the vaudeville art of Sir Harry Lauder and a host of lesser " Scotch comics " is still an easily marketable commodity; and if there was ever an assiduous cultivator of the Kailyard it was Harry Lauder —not forgetting the fact that in his heyday he was inspired by at least near-genius. (If the close critic of these matters looks for a toothsome theme, let him consider how Scots humour depends so much on denigration and the anticlimax. The line runs as clear as a scarlet thread from the writings of John Galt to the sketches of Will Fyffe. And the Sassenach still dotes on the spectacle of the Scot making a clumsy ass of himself!) The Scottish addiction to the intimate, pawky and canny is, moreover, confessed in various writings still in lively circulation.

It is perhaps safe to say, for instance, that Neil Munro, the exquisite romantic novelist of *The New Road*, *Gilian the Dreamer* and *Doom Castle*, is at this moment more popularly regarded for certain pieces he wrote under the pseudonym of "Hugh Foulis," a busy and brilliant journalist with the *Evening News* of Glasgow. That city's lively evening newspapers have always tended to favour the " sketch " with a strong local flavour, and especially the series built round a comic character with the gift of topical comment. Thus a worthy called " Jeems Kaye " for years delighted the readers of a defunct weekly, *The Bailie*.

This was tolerably crude stuff, but Munro elevated the

trick to a minor art. Some of his inventions are forgotten, except by the fond and ageing, but the anecdotes he built round the charming personality of "Para Handy" are deservedly alive and popular, their bantering humour and loving observation of the West Highland foibles still attractive. Strangers to the district might be surprised to find the skipper of a steam lighter and his crew paraded as typical of the region, but the steam lighter is to the Firth of Clyde what the sailing barge is to London River; and Munro was in this sense the Scottish W. W. Jacobs. And if there be any quarrel with my classification of the Para Handy pieces in the Kailyard group, the objector has surely failed to understand the issues of technique and approach involved. The difference is really that, in writing of a small world, and often in the inevitable haste of journalism, Munro's delicate and reticent personality saved him from the excesses of his elders.

In the early years of this twentieth century there began to appear in the *Evening Times* of Glasgow another series of "sketches" which, by their fidelity to the externalities of Clydeside life at least, immediately attracted the delighted attention of the regional public to whom they were addressed in the first place. They appeared at first over the modest initials of "J. J. B.," and these stood for John Joy Bell (1871-1934), the son of a considerable tobacco manufacturer, who made the commercial mistake of trying to stand out against the Imperial Tobacco Company, but whose name is still on the labels of a few brands.

Bell was thus born into comfort and affluence in the merchant order of society, was quite expensively educated, and was no doubt intended by his father for a seat on the board of a considerable business. But he would write; and it is remarkable that his observation of the working-class mind, tongue and society should have been so wholly exact and so unpatronizingly sympathetic. He had in these first sketches created the personality of "Wee Macgreegor." When the "sketches" came to be collected in book form, and John Hassall had invented a striking if absurd design for the cover, Joy Bell enjoyed for a space an immense commercial popularity in Britain and the United States—perhaps the last, wild wave of enthusiasm for a product of the Kailyard. It is sad to think, even if it may seem a thought irrelevant, that Bell, thanks to loose contracts with certain publishers, did not enjoy all the financial success that he had fairly won; for he was in person the sweetest, gentlest, most modest, most absurdly generous man you might find in a year of travelling.

Wee Macgreegor is the vivacious, inquisitive son of a Glasgow artisan and his decent wife, and the child's sayings and questions, in the dialect of the Clydeside, are the spring of the whole collection. The Robinsons move in a restricted circle; they visit respectable relations or the Zoo and, on a special occasion, enjoy a sail on the Firth of Clyde in the traditional Glasgow manner. It is all as simple as you please, inevitably sentimental, but some quality in it—of honesty, of veracity—gives it such an agreeable vitality that to this day it remains the favourite reading in many a Scottish nursery, at least. Though episodic, a collection of "pieces," it is of infinitely more perdurable stuff than, say, Crockett's more elaborately organized *Lilac Sunbonnet*, if only because it is blessedly free from the vices of patronage and exploitation.

It would be amusing to tell here and now the true story of the young J. J. Bell's first formal encounter with the established J. M. Barrie, but that must await a more suitable occasion. . . . Our interest must still be the persistence of the Kailyard strain in Scottish writing, long after Barrie,

Crockett and Watson had either retired from the scene or exhausted the wayward interest of the reading public.

As we have seen, the special popularity of the triumvirate lasted for rather less than ten years, from about 1888 until 1896. If Crockett and Watson continued to work the seam, with dwindling success, Barrie turned quickly enough to his proper business of a theatrical craftsman; and it is clear enough that the library public had had enough of dour and comic Scotch elders before Queen Victoria died. In another sort of study, which would have to be longer and subtler than this one, it would be useful to analyse those velleities of popular taste, and those influences upon it, that gave the Kailyard men their popularity and prosperity. No doubt some careful literary historian will some day (if the set of facts has not already been examined) explain to us why that enigmatic body, the library subscribers, turned quite quickly from sentimentalities to the new realisms of such as Shaw and Wells. For it is not as if the popularity of the Kailyard writers was like that of the works of Mrs. Florence L. Barclay, Miss Ethel M. Dell and Mr. A. S. M. Hutchinson. It is quite daunting to read to-day with what gravity the best weekly reviews of the period took Mr. Barrie's latest masterpieces. We have to consider hereabouts certain social and historical, as distinct from purely literary, phenomena.

Meanwhile, truly gifted Scots lingered among the runts in the cabbage-patch, declining to face the dreadful conditions and the state of mind industrialism in its fiercest form had imposed upon their country and their countrymen. The Kirk had never a bigger triumph of continuing influence! Both Neil Munro and J. J. Bell lived into the thirties of this century. John Buchan could not keep the Gorbals Die-Hards (impossible infants and pure products of a diet of curly greens) out of his most gentlemanly romances; and, once again, John Buchan was the son of a Free Kirk manse! The survivors of the original Free Church of Scotland should really try to account for their enormous and unfortunate influence on the normal development of Scottish letters.

Nor is it as if two World Wars and economic embarrassment in its most painful forms have succeeded in moving the mass of Scottish people from their allegiance to the old dream of a settled and mainly rural society. Some of the proofs of this point are surprising and not a little comic.

Many so-called Scottish newspapers are nowadays controlled, and virtually edited, from London, and of these controllers not a great deal of sympathy with the native point of view can be expected, unless, of course, an obvious commercial advantage accrues from the act of patronage. The "sketch" has tended to disappear even from Glasgow's evening sheets, nowadays reduced to the current level of standardization by the devotion to "news value." Even so, it is notable that the reminiscences of old-timers are still favoured; the Scot, *laudator temporis acti*, still yearning to enjoy that old dream of his, will endlessly consume the records and debate the historicity of landmarks and "characters." It is even more to the point that one of the most highly-successful and efficient periodical publishing firms in Scotland, the Thomson-Leng firm of Dundee, flourishes largely by the careful cultivation of the Kailyard strain.

This organization—and its sense of Scottish popular taste is almost always unerring—publishes *inter alia* a number of weeklies designed to please those who still sit about the domestic fireside and regard its clime as the most agreeable within human reach. The *People's Friend*, the *Red Letter* and the *People's Journal* are typical titles, carrying an almost Biblical authority into thousands of Scottish homes. The recipe varies according to a very nice understanding of class-distinctions and tastes, but no Thomson-Leng editor would dare to ignore the supreme importance of the sketch, the short story and the serial; and these are in the Kailyard mode invariably, even if the setting is not always rural. The cartoons and " strips " themselves must take the homely line without fail. The appeal to the simple human heart, rather than to the complicated and bemused human mind, is emphasized; and the woman in the home is the main target of this adroit journalism.

It was in this field that the valorous Annie S. Swan chiefly laboured and most greatly prospered. No writer has ever so perfectly matched her chosen publisher's hour. But Mrs. Burnett-Smith did not, at least, pretend to unique cleverness, was never guilty of overdoing either the dialect or the pawkiness, and regarded herself simply as (what she was) a competent writer of simple, sentimental tales for the commercial market. She was the queen of a considerable tribe of females that still flourishes on the supply of a steady demand.

It is amusing enough to note the persistence of the Kailyard *motif* even in the operations of the Scottish Region of the British Broadcasting Corporation. The Drama department of that body has done first-rate work in giving a wide hearing to plays and poetic adventures that might otherwise have waited long enough for recognition by commercial persons, but it is a fact that the Scottish B.B.C.'s prize silver teapot, the joy of a considerable majority of its listeners, is a regular " feature " programme entitled " The McFlannels."

This is a series of dramatized sketches that has been running now for many years, with summer breaks; and it is pure

Kailyard. The capable authoress, Mrs. Helen W. Pryde, has conceived a Glasgow family on the social level that might once upon a time have been safely described as somewhere between the superior artisan and the lower middle-class strata. During the war years its means and status have advanced, and much of the fun rests on the first encounters of simple folk with social pretensions more spacious than those to which they have been accustomed. (The shrewd reader will note the inevitable Kailyard trick of playing on the acute Scottish awareness of distinctions of class, wealth and manners.) Mrs. Pryde is excellent on local speech; she and her actors can get exactly the intonations of a Glasgow family on the way from tenement flat to bungalow; she observes the rubs and foibles of family life both acutely and kindly. What is chiefly interesting about this blameless work is its recurrent demonstration of one of the prime Kailyard faults—such an indifference to the form and construction of an anecdote that, when poor Mrs. Pryde has established quite a promising situation and then becomes aware of the merciless ticking of the studio clock, she is ruthless in cutting corners and sacrificing probability in order to get her creatures off the floor within the stipulated thirty minutes.

It is still more interesting, and much more to the point of our study, that this somewhat vestigial phenomenon, as it might be the ghost of the early J. J. Bell, has such a vogue among the Scots nearly a hundred years after the birth of William Robertson Nicoll.

If, however, we incline in our modern superiority to imagine that the commercial success of the Kailyard writers was among the nitwits only we make a serious mistake. Once again we must marvel that Barrie, Crockett and Watson were not applauded merely by the sort of people who, in later times, guaranteed the substantial fortunes of Mrs. Barclay and Miss Dell. Their appeal was apparently to the quite " intelligent " reader of the sort that, in a more recent period, read, discussed and delighted in the works of, say, Hugh Walpole and Francis Brett Young. Their books were bought by the best people in the West End, borrowed from the most fashionable circulating libraries. The responsible reviewers of the age accorded them great respect.

Scotland's two leading newspapers, the *Glasgow Herald* and the *Scotsman*, received the works with gravity, if with native caution, but it is even more remarkable that the leading weeklies of the period—the *Athenaeum*, the *Spectator* and so on—dealt with them at length and solemnly, especially in the case of Barrie. Those were, indeed, the days of dignified reviewing, of a critical style as heavy and ornate as a Victorian bedroom suite, but it is extremely difficult to discover any contemporary sign of suspicion that these confections from the North were perhaps a trifle bogus, partial and, most obviously, sentimentalized. It was as if, in England, people were only beginning to discover Scotland as a strange sort of place and revelling in this parade of the comic inwardness of Scottish life. And the Kailyard authors never failed to minister subtly to the powerful English instinct for the patronage of lesser breeds without the law.

Only one substantial bomb fell anywhere near the cultivators of the Caledonian vineyard in their heyday. It did them very little harm and, so far as one can discern, completely failed to shake the faith of those who bought and borrowed the books in such satisfactory numbers. This was the article J. H. Millar contributed to Henley's *New Review*. It may be found in a few good reference libraries on page 384 of Volume 12 of that defunct periodical, January-June, 1895.

There is some piquancy in its appearance under Henley's editorship, for Barrie had been an occasional contributor to his *Scots Review*. There is still more piquancy in the quality of the article, for although Millar was a professorial sort of person, he laid about him with a heavy blade and most searchingly made those points of attack on the Kailyard position which are so much easier to make in these later times, when the illusion has been torn to shreds by several sets of circumstances.

Here he is in full flight, taking (be it remembered) his young head in his hands against the armies commanded by such as Robertson Nicoll:

> " It is a fact that J. M. Barrie is fairly entitled to look upon himself as *pars magna*, if not *pars maxima*, of the great Kailyard movement. If to-day in Scotland hardly the humblest rag is without its study of native life, and if ne'er a Free Kirk probationer, too modest to aspire to the smug heresies and complacent latitudinarianism of its teachers, but manfully resolves that he too will storm the world with his 'Cameos from the Cowcaddens' or his 'Glimpses of the Goose-dubs,' it is Mr. Barrie's doing. . . . The Chronicles of the Kailyard are ill at ease in the flower garden."

One may discern in this passage something of a denominational prejudice, but it was bravely said, and the modern Scot must salute Millar as one who, early in the proceedings, objected to the Kailyard version of Scottish life as a crude betrayal of the national dignity.

Using a weapon with a sharper edge, Millar repeated and, with more material to work on, amplified his charges in his *History of Scottish Literature*, seven years later. To his memory must go such credit as may accrue to the first substantial critic to attack the Kailyard position on a solid front. This credit is usually given, in error, to a strange and able man, George Douglas Brown (1869–1902), author of that landmark in Scottish fiction, *The House with the Green Shutters*.

Like Crockett, Brown was born the bastard son of a farmer. This was in the townlet of Ochiltree in Ayrshire, which lies not so far from Boswell's paternal Auchinleck in a tolerably rich agricultural countryside that is curiously diversified by the bings and gantries of coal workings. Of his mother Brown could say in his manhood that she was " a good and religious woman, but she was just an uneducated, short-coated peasant," and the circumstances of his birth may have had their bearing on the development of an austere, even glum, personality. The photographs taken in the hour of his success reveal a chronic scowl. On his father's side, however, was an inheritance of literary and linguistic ability, and the boy was a good scholar. After passing through two village schools he was assisted to Ayr Academy and thence won a bursary to Glasgow University; and there he graduated M.A. with Honours in Classics in 1890. In the same year he won the Eglinton Fellowship of £100 for three years; and in the next he was awarded a Snell Exhibition of £130 for three years at Balliol College, Oxford—an honour rightly regarded as one of the plums of scholarship in Scotland.

It must be explained here that both the biographical and bibliographical material concerning this strange figure are unsatisfactory. The standard work of reference is now the Memorial Edition of *The House with the Green Shutters*, published in 1923 by Brown's friend, Andrew Melrose. This starts unhappily with the confession that " owing to various circumstances accurate information as to the several previous editions is not available," and it ends with a biographical sketch and some personal reminiscences from Mr. Melrose's pen, which can fairly be described as warm-hearted but rather woolly; and it may be, indeed, that Brown's reticence contributed not a little to the vagueness of these pieces in so far as facts and dates are concerned.

At all events, proceeding to Oxford with a Snell in 1891, the young man would appear to have had fine prospects, but it is clear that he and Oxford did not agree very well. He was older than most of the students about him, the climate did not suit him, and we may guess that his stern temperament failed to accommodate itself to the easy English assumptions. Much more than that, however, it is possible to guess from Mr. Melrose's evidence that Brown had developed by this time that sense of destiny which drove him to the ultimate, tardy production of his one, fine book—the sense that he deserved and must duly earn the title of "man of letters." He insisted in unlikely circumstances on the formal use of this phrase. So he did not work hard at Oxford, was not assimilated into its life and traditions, and, without formally accepting the degree he had won, left in 1895 to follow the path worn by thousands of gifted young Scots towards Fleet Street and fortune.

It appears that Brown's struggle was a hard one, and we may safely conjecture that a man of his austere temperament did not easily make those adjustments which freelance journalism demands of its uneasy practitioners. A short story here and there, two "hack" books for boys under different pseudonyms, a little book reviewing, an odd paragraph—the graph of the pilgrim's progress is familiar; and in Brown Scotland had not sent another Barrie into Grub Street. The determination was there, however. Mr. Melrose tells how an essay on Burns was accepted for *Blackwood's Magazine* and drew from the publishers an invitation to Brown to present himself in Edinburgh—and this promising opportunity was not taken. On another occasion some of his friends bespoke for him a substantial appointment for which he was academically well-qualified, and he would have none of it. He was determined to succeed in the traditional way as a Man of Letters.

Making allowances for Mr. Melrose's pardonable pride in his own part in the shaping of Brown and his only book, we do gather that the angular Scot was steadied and heartened when, in 1898 or thereabouts, he met Howard Spicer, then editor of *Sandow's Magazine*, and, through Spicer, Melrose himself. These three, all with careers still to make, formed an earnest sodality in which literature and ideas were endlessly discussed in the traditional way of the ambitious and intelligent young. We get the impression of Brown as a brilliant and forceful talker when in the mood, capable of menacing silences. It is touching to read how his purpose to become a real man of letters remained steady and was duly accepted and encouraged by his friends and how, when he hit upon his theme, the work in progress was the subject of continual debate.

We shall have to consider in a moment or two how far *The House with the Green Shutters* was deliberately organized as a counterblast to the excessive sentimentality of the Kailyard men. As intelligent Scots, both Brown and Melrose despised the attitude, and we may fairly imagine that Brown's inner conviction of power and his lack of success combined to make him feel a thought sore towards Barrie, Crockett and Co. In the meantime, it is most interesting to know that the famous novel was first written as a long short story of some 20,000 words, and that it was expanded to its ultimate 80,000 as the result (if we follow Mr. Melrose) of earnest discussions among the three friends. This, I think, is the key to certain obvious faults of the technical kind in the completed work. One may at least hazard the suggestion that it might have been a more perfect novel, in both shape and balance of emphasis, if Brown had conceived it as a full-length novel in the first place and worked on it according to his own exclusive lights. It was, however, duly finished, accepted and published in both Britain and the United States in the late autumn of 1901.

The publishing history of *The House with the Green Shutters* is an odd one. Mr. Melrose is less than lucid as to the details, but there seems to have been some hitch in the appearance of the English edition (by McQueen, of Bury Street, Bloomsbury), and the reviews came tardily. The two great Scottish newspapers dealt with it promptly and seriously. Brown was pleased to find the *Glasgow Herald* describe it as " True to the verge of being merciless. . . . If we smile, it is at the cruel point of some stinging jest. . . . Overdrawn, but grimly true, and full of promise "—and that was, in fact, a very just contemporary opinion. He was equally pleased that the *Scotsman* " put it first in their list of fiction," but indignant to have it described by that eminent sheet as " brutally coarse." There were good notices in the *Pall Mall Gazette* and other places, but Brown's first novel, so momentous in his serious sense of mission, showed no sign of being popularly recognized as anything but the average first novel until, miraculously and belatedly, Andrew Lang praised it highly in *Longman's Magazine*.

Lang was the grand vizier of reviewing in those days. The small fry jumped to the lifting of his forefinger. He was also that recurrent phenomenon, the multiple reviewer. Soon *The Times* and the *Morning Post* were praising this strange and powerful tale of Scottish life; the chorus was taken up everywhere. Quickly enough the innocent British public, which had so gladly accepted the Rev. Dr. Watson's toothsome anecdotes as true and charming pictures of Scottish life, was now rejoicing with the appropriate shivers in a tale of Scottish small-town life, in which few prospects pleased and man was quite remarkably and consistently vile. It must have seemed to the few detached that it was nearly impossible for any Scot to take his own country and countrymen with moderation, equally impossible for any Englishman or American to conceive the existence North of the Tweed of any reasonably well-balanced person—excluding, of course, the occupant of the local Free Kirk manse. . . . In that context, it is interesting that Brown does not anywhere in his one remarkable novel mention the Kirk or the Minister. This, in an Ayrshire Scotsman, must be reckoned a staggering feat of self-denial and, what is much more to the point, artistic reticence.

So George Douglas Brown arrived. (The novel was first published as being by " George Douglas.") Mr. Melrose has a touching anecdote to illustrate the man's severe pride in his success. They went together to a London bank to deposit the first considerable cheque for royalties earned in the United States, and Melrose, who was conducting the business, described Brown to the bank's officer as " a novelist." Brown intervened, saying gravely: " No. Man of letters." And we need not smirk at what seems a priggish pose. He had dreamed long and worked hard to earn the lovely laurels.

But what, now, about this novel that made literary history?

The plot is in the simplest convention of tragedy. John Gourlay, grain merchant and contractor in Barbie, dominates the township and its people, including the Provost and councillors, by his commercial success and the force of a ruthless personality. His house with the green shutters, overlooking the place, is the prized symbol of his brutal sovereignty. The capital for his enterprises came with his wife, but she is a feckless slut by the time we first meet her. The only son, young John, is a cocky coward, spoiled by his mother and mortally afraid, while proud, of his father. There is a daughter of whom Brown makes nothing except a figure of convenience in the last chapter.

A native of Barbie, named Wilson, returns with some commercial experience elsewhere and some capital, and Gourlay grossly insults him at the first encounter. Wilson, thus stung into rivalry, is cleverer than Gourlay by far. Cunningly managed, his new business takes trade from Gourlay until the house with the green shutters is ultimately all the man has left to mask his pride. He is represented as being so fierce in his lust for power and prominence that, when he hears of Wilson's son going to the university, he must send his own John the same way, even if the lad is ill-fitted for the vocation and was destined to be the natural successor to a triumphant business.

Young John makes a mess of things at Edinburgh, learns to drink to almost incredible excess, and is sent down. His return in this disgrace coincides with Gourlay's final realization of his commercial failure and, therefore, the collapse of his pride. There is the inevitable scene between father and son, and a blow is struck with a poker. The death of the old man is represented as a fall on to the edge of the fender, but remorse and fear have their way with young John; he indulges in a bout of drinking and then in a dram of poison. Mother and sister, the latter now a hopeless invalid, discover in their terror that there is still poison in the bottle and share it in a last pact of death. The house with the green shutters is finally the mortuary of the Gourlays and their pride.

It may read crudely enough in this version, but Brown carried it off. Even if the consumptive daughter, of whom we have heard next to nothing beforehand, is dragged in at the end by the hair of the head to make the fatal decision, the horror of the affair is not abated by that technical consideration. The character of old Gourlay is wildly improbable, we may say in the forenoon, but in the lamplight it frightens as much as it frightened his weakling son. The tale of technical blemishes may be long enough. Brown all too often falls into the beginner's vice of explaining his characters as from author to reader instead of suffering them to explain themselves in thought, speech and action; and, even so, Brown's discourses on his own characters and on the Scottish character in general are packed with arresting aphorisms. Many readers may share my feeling that the passages on young Gourlay's life at Edinburgh University and, in particular, his surrender to extremely large libations of strong drink are both clotted and scamped—probably one of those extensions fitted on to the original short story; but the suspension of disbelief is only mildly shaken. Brown carries it all off by a force almost as ruthless as that which he makes us believe old Gourlay to have possessed.

The high merits of the book are clear. First of all, the sheer gift of story-telling, the natural drive of the born novelist, for which there can be no accounting. Next, a surprisingly tender feeling for the " atmosphere " of a small country town, particularly (as the critical and sensitive reader may be interested to note and check) in the early hours of fine spring and summer mornings. Third, an extraordinarily efficient and yet perfectly natural use of dialect, especially in its personal applications. But the supreme literary virtue of the tragedy is Brown's brilliant success in the presentation and characterization of his Greek Chorus—the " bodies " of Barbie. Here we have at once his finest creative success and his most effective criticism of the sentimental tendencies of Crockett and Watson at least. As I hope to be able to show, Brown and Barrie were not so terribly far apart in their attitude to the peasant Scot as some may think.

The " bodies " of any Scottish village are—or, rather, used to be—the equivalent of the " gaffers " in the English tradition. They were those male inhabitants of small places who could afford the time to gather round the village pump or its equivalent, even in the forenoon, watch what was going on, speculate on motives, exchange small rumours, pass on malicious gossip and act in general as the clearing-house of local news.

The bus and the popular Press have changed all that by now, but such people had a curiously powerful influence, often malignant enough, on the social atmosphere of any small and isolated community in the middle decades of the nineteenth century. It is one of the supreme virtues of *The House with the Green Shutters* that Brown gives this social factor prominence, making his group of " bodies " at the Bend o' the Brae participants in the drama as well as spectators of the central tragedy. They watch and speculate and put two and two together (usually making five) and they are a repulsive bunch of small-town malignants, but Brown, handling their snivelling dialect with mastery, shows that the negative force they wield is as much a factor in the downfall of a masterful man as Gourlay's unrelenting pride.

And is Scotland really like that? the non-Scottish reader may fairly ask now. Given the period and the circumstance of rural isolation in the mid-nineteenth century, is Brown's picture not as one-sided in its way as Watson's? The answers to these questions require of us some nice distinctions.

Clearly, Brown was every bit as guilty as the Kailyard men of holding his fellow-countrymen up to the ridicule of the foreigner: his only possible defence being, in the boyish phrase, " but they started it." It must also be maintained that he is, in one direction, as false to the facts of Scottish life (or any other sort of peasant life) as Crockett. The pity inherent in his tragic conception apart, there is precious little acknowledgment of the kindness, sentiment and tenderness of the ordinary life in *The House with the Green Shutters.* The jests are of the bitterest variety. There is no honest laughter in Barbie, only a nasty whinnying of small persons. We accept Brown's world while he has us in his charge as a storyteller, but we hesitate, in the early hours of the next morning, to accept his premisses.

Now, the documentary values of fiction may be nothing as beside the power of the novelist to induce in us that willing suspension of disbelief, but here we must concern ourselves with claims that have been widely made as to the importance of Brown's one novel in relation to the Kailyard success. It is still said, sometimes by people who should know better, that it blasted the Kailyard seedlings overnight; and that is to ignore the clear fact that the Kailyard was bound to wither in the changing social and scientific conditions of the early twentieth century. In his pardonable pride in his influence on Brown while the tale was being written, Mr. Melrose makes it out to have been conceived in almost direct reaction to the Kailyard interpretation of Scottish life. Brown was determined to display the other side of the shield, " the Scot malignant." Therefore, Mr. Melrose implies, his friend wrote *The House with the Green Shutters.*

This is nonsense, surely. One must refuse to believe that any considerable work of the creative order—and *The House with the Green Shutters* is certainly that—can be produced as a sort of polemic, a mere retort like any Letter to the Editor. I am myself confident in the view that, however much Brown's genius may have been stimulated by the success of what he thought to be worthless and false, and by his earnest friends, *The House with the Green Shutters* was the novel he was born and bound to write, the grim story that had long been gestating within a wry and awkward personality: the chunk of convinced, inward truth that fortified a shy man in claiming the title of Man of Letters.

One last thought has its fascination. Of Barrie's attitude to rural life in Scotland one has used that hard word "sadism." Of George Douglas Brown's testimony on the same subject one could reasonably use the word "brutal" or, at the least, "merciless." The distinction is all-important in any understanding of the Kailyard betrayal, as the modern Scot sees it. One writes of Barrie in his Kailyard phase as a sadist because, so obviously the master of technique and understanding, he sniggered, nudged with the elbow, whispered under his hand, and exploited the intimacies of his most private life to make the picture appealing to those who might buy it. Brown was cruel, but he was as honest as the bright mornings he so loved to describe. He was possessed of a savage indignation indeed, but he did not drag the short-coated peasant, who was his mother, into the proceedings. He saw his world from the outside, honestly if clumsily at times, and, though lacking Barrie's exquisite gift of presentation, slugged away to give us what he believed to be a neglected facet of truth. His one novel remains in the classic order of such things. We need not imagine that the best of Barrie will die before the only flower of Brown's genius, but we may safely believe that *The House with the Green Shutters* will live as long as literate men are capable of saying: " Yes, but look at this side of the picture."

We may wonder what Brown might have gone on to do had he survived, but the evidence is disappointing. On August 28, 1902, he died after a brief illness, apparently something in the nature of a cerebral haemorrhage; and Mr. Melrose can only testify that his friend planned to write next a romantic love-story of the Cromwellian period —which sounds a very unpromising theme for the author of *The House with the Green Shutters* !—and then a story with the rather more reassuring title of *The Incompatibles*. Now he is in literary history that occasional, fascinating phenomenon—a writer with a big reputation based on a single book that was remarkable in its period and a turning point in a national literary process at least.

As has been consistently argued in these pages, it is a misunderstanding of the facts to credit Brown wholly with the blasting of the pretty plants in the Kailyard. That was coming inevitably through natural causes. His function was to administer the *coup de grâce* in the single blow that is all we know him to have been capable of. Since *The House with the Green Shutters* appeared nearly fifty years ago, no Scot of any real literary ability but has been forced to consider his attitude to his own people in the light of Brown's demonstration.

The last word was probably with Brown's old teacher at Glasgow University, that Walter Raleigh, who liked neither the human race nor its silly face, and wrote:

> I love the book for just this, it sticks the Kailyarders like pigs.

Thus ended one queer phase in the history of popular taste in these British Isles.

THE END

INDEX